Life Mapping

A Journey of Self Discovery
and
Path Finding

By

Monika Moss-Gransberry

Keys For Life Publishing

Cleveland, Ohio

Life Mapping – A Journey of Self Discovery and Path Finding

by Monika Moss-Gransberry

ISBN- 978-0-9849520-2-1

Published by Rolands Press and Keys For Life Publishing,

Cleveland, Ohio

For information, address Keys For Life Publishing, 11470 Euclid Avenue Cleveland Ohio 44106.

Edited by Tamara Jeffries, Connie Atkins, Becky Norwood

Publishing Advisors: Spotlight Publishing™

Cover Art by Tunde Afolayan

Table of Contents

PREFACE

I Am Grateful

Now I understand why writers thank so many people when they have finally completed a book. This book has been a labor of love. I have learned so much about commitment during this process. I have learned about clarity. I learned how to be clear and honest with myself. More than anything, I have learned about support.

Throughout this process, I have been supported by so many people. Without their loving and challenging support, I could not have completed this leg of my journey. I could not have followed my map to the completion of this book.

There are so many people who have shaped the person that I am and thus this book's content. The people who have been instrumental in my life are far too numerous to mention. All have enriched my life through each relationship and the lessons they taught.

I want to thank all of my clients who have entrusted me to support them in mapping out their vision and a road to get there. I want to thank all the people who believed in me, who gave me a chance, who took care of me, who put up with me, who pushed me, who comforted me, who sat with me, who watched from afar, who tagged along, who showed up fully, who taught me and who loved me each in their own way.

I want to thank John Harris, John Carter, Everett Gransberry, Gayle Agahi, Rodney Robinson, Kenneth Robinson, Roland Robinson, May & Paul Haugstad, Donald & Camilla Moss, Candace Sheffler, Veronica Moss-Naysmith, Bernice &

Willa Mae Robinson, Nina Simmons, Marie Zieger, Woodie King Jr., Sharon Groves-Marsh, The Women of Wealth, Wendy Bowers-Cherry-Ellis, Kim Bey, Christina Graf, Ed Spriggs, Felton Eaddy, Isabel Wong, Mauricio Puerto, John & Veronica Carter, The Gestalt Institute of Cleveland and the Gestalt OSD Center, Sondra McCurry, Alsie Clay, Renee Whiteside, Rachel Chapman, Greer Jordan, Debbi Mayo, Women of Wolf Creek, Laura Chapman, Will Scott, Nolan Shaw, Tony Bennae Richard, Paul Hill Jr., Montrie Rucker, Kathryn Hall, Connie Atkins, Roderick Redus, Tunde Afolayan, and Tamara Jeffries.

Above all, I am grateful to the Universe for sending me all of the lessons, the wisdom, and the experiences that have allowed me to learn this way of being called Life Mapping and to share it with you. Thank you all for your support and love and faith in me.

Special New Edition Update

I was inspired to update this book with the launch of my new book, *The Technology of Doing Creating & Being: Engineering the Transformation of your Life Using Self-mastery as the Spiritual Blueprint*. This book documents my new learning. And it just felt right to take a look at this book and offer some updates. And to my pleasure, as I reread the book, so much of everything here is congruent and aligned with my evolved thinking and experience. This book is still foundational to everything you want to create for yourself. It is one way to find clarity and a path for moving forward.

Today, I am always asking the question: What is needed now? And in the updating and reviewing of this book, I was affirmed that this is what is needed now for so many who are looking to be more intentional and authentic in life's journey or for those who are stuck and looking to jump-start or reinvent their vision for themselves and manifest a new life.

Enjoy and grow within as you read and explore your own path inspired by the words and the exercises and ideas I have shared here in this book.

Allow yourself to be inspired and find joy.

Allow yourself to see a way, find the path, and happily move forward on your journey.

Allow yourself to aspire to better health, more happiness, and wholeness.

INTRODUCTION

"Most people search high and wide for the key to success. If they only knew the key to their dreams lies within."
--George Washington Carver- inventor, and educator

Life Mapping is an inner journey. The key to your ideal lifestyle lies within you. Your vision, your commitment, your ability to adapt to both inner and outer change, all factors into your ability to live your ideal lifestyle and manifest the life you will love to live right now. The goal of this book is to help you clarify your vision, strengthen your commitment and create and respond to the changes that will impact your life.

Life is a journey both literally and metaphorically. We are constantly moving from the thought process to the day-to-day doing. We are changing and growing — mentally, emotionally and spiritually. And we're traveling our personal highways of life whether we have a map or not. One day dissolves into the next, week after week, month after month. Our lives get lived. And we are making choices all along the way. In every step, every thought, every action, we are making choices. Some people say they just follow the road wherever it takes them—but even that is a choice. Life Mapping gives us a more considered direction and helps us make conscious choices.

The Beginning ...

While I was a struggling graduate student in New York City, I saw an ad in the paper for a training manager and a part-time consultant position at an agency that provided management training to nonprofit organizations. I interviewed for the consulting job and became the training manager responsible for planning and coordinating two annual workshop series using volunteer trainers from the business community. Supporting presenter(s) with their design and creating, copying and collating handouts—in the days before automatic sorters. I spent many evenings reading and hand collating materials for workshops over Chinese take-out and a cold beer.

It was through the Support Center that I met Marie, Executive Director for the New Jersey center, who became my mentor and friend. And through working with her, I consciously began my journey as a consultant. Marie was short-handed in the New Jersey office and asked me to help her after hours. I had taken her 'Making Meetings Work' workshop and we talked often about the importance of facilitation. Finally, she asked if I'd like to assist her as a facilitator. I jumped at the opportunity. That was the beginning. After that, we partnered several times. Then, she began to send me out with clients on my own, supporting me in my design and helping me think through my approach and strategy. It was in that paneled office in Newark, NJ that I was becoming a consultant.

One day after I'd been working with her for a couple of years, Marie and I locked ourselves up in the conference room at the office on a Saturday morning. Our plan was to help each other develop a focus and direction for our personal and professional lives. We were both struggling with how to make our dreams come true. The fear, discomfort, and potential of our situation begged action. So, early that Saturday morning, we gathered ourselves together at the office. The sun brightened the room as we cleared last week's flip chart paper off the wood-paneled walls in preparation for doing our personal work.

By that time, I had become a full-fledged management consultant freelancing with the agency. With the never-ending energy of youth, I was also working in a theatre where I did various jobs from box office to sound and props to producing a late-night cabaret. In addition, I had started working as an artist manager for several emerging artists. So there I was a year after graduate school with lots of ideas, too many projects, no money, and a long-term relationship, wondering what I wanted to be when I really grew up. I wanted it all. But I wasn't sure how to get it.

We figured that we ought to be able to translate the approach we used with our clients into a form that would work for us personally. We asked our strategic planning clients to identify their values, envision an ideal future and explore their strengths and weaknesses, and we helped them create strategies to move their organizations towards their vision. Marie and I asked each other the same questions, articulating our personal visions for the future and looking at the gap between that vision and our current reality. We asked ourselves what was keeping us from having our vision now and developed some beginning strategies to help us reach our goals.

When we left the room that evening, we each had a clear vision and strategies for getting there. This was my first experience with what I now refer to as Life Mapping.

Life Mapping is a process for envisioning the life you want and figuring out how to live it. Life Mapping is about discovering and rediscovering the things that are most important to you, committing to them (and yourself) and then watching those things manifest as you move on life's journey and fulfill your commitment to the One who made us all- The Universe, The Creator, The Great Spirit, Mother Earth, The One with Many Names or simply, God.

For the past twenty years, I have been living, modifying, forgetting about and manifesting my Life Map. This synchronicity has been amazing. Even when I thought I'd abandoned pieces of my dream, they later resurfaced—often to my amazement—inspiring renewed focus and commitment.

Even when I was unsure, even when I forgot about my dreams, I had set in motion something very powerful that continued to come back to me. Each year I revisit and update my Life Map as things around me changed and as I changed and evolved. The more I focused on the vision I set, the more things seemed to fall into place creating exactly what I had asked for. And then I would change my mind or come to realize that I needed something a bit different.

It was these detours that have created my real understanding of what gets in the way of my dreams and other people's dreams. In that conference room with Marie, we had just scratched the surface of what Life Mapping is and what is really needed for you to manifest your dreams in a way that you can enjoy them. There was a need to go much deeper into the meaning and motivation behind the dream and to clearly articulate and move through all the stuff that confuses our thinking and gets in our way. It has taken twenty years for me to bring Life Mapping to this point and be ready to share it with you.

The Intention of Life Mapping and This Book

This book is the essence of my thinking and learning about how mapping or creating a life map can be an effective tool for personal development. It includes ideas and lessons that I have found profound and extremely useful in my journey and the journeys of others as they have shared their experiences with me.

Over the years, I've learned the truth in that old saying: "Be careful what you ask for, you just might get it." I found that you are *guaranteed* to get it—one way or the other.

Our thoughts, words, and desires have energy and power that are not to be taken lightly. They directly affect what manifests in our lives. Religious leaders, philosophers, and now even neuroscientists understand that what goes on in our minds comes to fruition in our bodies and in our lives. Before you say, "I want a fancy house. I want a better job. I want a new relationship," it's wise to explore exactly what the answer to that request may look like, what it means to you and how it will serve your larger life's purpose. A fancy house may end up being a headache to maintain. A new relationship—if that relationship is with a human being—will bring its own set of challenges.

So, you may be thinking, if you're going to get what you ask for, why bother with a Life Map? Well, you want to make sure you're clear about what you're asking for. You want to discern what you want from what you have been told to want by the media, relatives, and society. You want to make sure what you ask for today is in alignment with what you want for your future.

The purpose of a life map is CLARITY so you can create the most direct path to manifesting your vision and those things that are really important to you. It helps you to clear your mind. It's about shifting your thinking so that your energies are focused on what's needed and not the gazillion other things that may compete for your attention.

Life Mapping helps you cultivate the discipline to focus your thoughts, words, and actions in ways that contribute to creating what you really want and need instead of roaming around aimlessly, stumbling over roadblocks to your dreams. The more strategic you are in this endeavor, the faster you are likely to attain what you want in time to enjoy it. And part of enjoying it is recognizing that you got what you wanted.

Of course, as you set out on this kind of journey, you're going to stumble across road construction, detours, and other obstacles, just as you would on any road trip—no matter how hard you try not to. Some of these obstacles are external: things you have no control over, like a pothole in the road. Others are internal blocks: things that keep you from choosing the path you desire or from moving forward on your journey, like when you know you're lost but refuse to ask for directions. *Life Mapping* acknowledges that sometimes even the best plans go off course. When this happens, your life map offers you a way to look at the whole landscape as well as your own stretch of the road so that you see how to take the necessary detours and still get to your ultimate destination.

As you read this book and begin the *Life Mapping* process, keep in mind that this process is about *choices*—not only the choices that are presented to you by the road or terrain but the expanded choices you offer yourself which are created by how you choose to navigate the road ahead, by what vehicle you select, and what passengers you choose to accompany you.

This book is designed as a workbook. The idea is that you will do the exercises as you go; and by the time you are finished, you will have a map to guide you to your ideal lifestyle. Some of what you may learn is that you can get much of what you want instantly by simply changing your mind and doing something different. Some other things will take more time and effort.

If you read this book and are inspired to create and articulate your own life map, I will be thrilled. If you finish this book with new levels of clarity about your destination or some ideas about what's standing in your way, I am blessed to have served you well. If you discover some concrete strategies to help you work with those blocks so that you continue moving forward, then I have fulfilled my purpose. But ultimately this is about your own choices, your own happiness, and your own life's purpose. It's about working to get you where you want to be. I hope that you will find value in the sharing of these lessons as you continue on your journey.

It is in choosing that we exercise our freedom of choice, the one thing that separates us from other animals. In creating more choices for ourselves than the ones our parents had, or the limited choices society offers, we chose to be free. I wish you the freedom to choose and the power to map your future and make your vision real.

Your Expectations of the Process

How Life Mapping Works

The process of *Life Mapping* is as good as you make it. It's as valuable as you are honest with yourself. It is as effective as you are disciplined. In other words, this book will work for you, but it will not *do* your work for you. It will offer methods for doing the work. Included among the basic building blocks of Life Mapping are exercises and other tools that might be useful to you such as specific meditations, affirmations, and journal writing exercises that will encourage you to explore more fully all that you are and have the potential to be. In it, you'll also find stories and essays about other people's experiences on their life journey.

My hope is that these stories will inspire you and help you develop your own map. And through your work and your reading, you will see how this process is of value to you. You will find out more about yourself and your thinking. You will discover how your thinking impacts your choices and ability to make your visions real. You will walk into the uncharted territories of your mind and spirit. You will learn new things about yourself so that you can expand your range of being and your choices of how you show up in the world.

However, it's not always easy nor comfortable to chart new territory. You may find yourself wanting to turn away or go back. When you feel discomfort—whether it's anxiety, anger, annoyance—you may have gotten in touch with some new awareness or be on the verge of some new discovery in some new and unfamiliar place in the world or within yourself. Pay attention to these moments and sit with them. Let them show you the wisdom of your own intuition and feelings.

Let the exercises and the affirmations in the book support you during these moments. But don't stop, don't give up. **Remember:** It was no accident that this book caught your attention. There is a reason you were drawn to it. A good reason. You only have to keep reading to find out what it is. You are sure to discover the lessons and blessings that this experience holds for you.

Above all, take your time with this book and the process of Life Mapping. You wouldn't plan your dream vacation in an hour; you certainly want to take your time in planning the rest of your life. Allow for things to unfold in their own time. Keep your choices open until you are clear about which road will get you to the next intersection. And remember, there are rest stops, and way stations along the way that allow us to regroup, renew our energy and re-commit to the journey.

This is a book that I hope will become ragged and worn from use. Get all that you can out of this book and out of your life. Good luck on your journey.

CHAPTER 1: ORIENTEERING

Divine Love is doing its perfect work in my life.

A map, a compass, and a destination. That's all you get. You start out in the middle of the woods with a small team, you're given a map and a compass, and you have to find your way out of the forest. That's the premise of the sport called orienteering. It's often called the "thinking sport" because it involves not only cross-country racing, but topography navigation, map reading, and decision-making. The goal: to use the tools you've been given (including your team and your own sense of direction) to find your way from point A to point B... and ultimately to point Z, as fast as you can.

For some people, the idea of being literally "lost in the woods" may not sound like much fun. Yet if you knew you had the tools you needed, knew you had the knowledge and skill to find our way, knew that you were certain to reach your destination—and if you learned to see the process as meaningful and enjoyable—well, it wouldn't seem so bad, would it? If you knew you'd succeed, and be stronger and wiser, in the end, you might just find pleasure in the process.

The same goes for life's journey. Many of us find ourselves in the middle of nowhere, lost and confused, but with the right tools and the right approach, you can find your way out of the proverbial woods. When you look at it that way, orienteering is a great metaphor for the process of finding your way in life. Orienteering is a great metaphor for Life Mapping because what orienteering offers as a physical and mental exercise, Life Mapping offers to your life in general.

Life Mapping is a process designed to help you find focus and direction in your life, to concentrate your energies and efforts on what you want and need, to create a clear vision for your future and a map to lead you to that destination, and to find the motivation you need in order to reach your goal. If you know where you are headed and why, then no matter what curves life throws at you, you can stay focused and keep yourself oriented in that direction. If you have a life map, detours won't worry you. (You may even take some intentional side trips because you know, ultimately, what you are working toward.)

Life Mapping is a way to choice-fully find a path to what brings you the most fulfillment. When you follow your heart's desires, your spirit's yearnings; when you zero in on what you really want; you not only find your path, but you can change your world into one more perfectly suited for you. Then you can begin living the lifestyle you envision.

Like enthusiasts of orienteering, we each face challenges and obstacles in navigating our way to our destination, enjoying the paradox of having a map and navigational tools, but also dealing with the unexpected twists and turns that the journey—even a carefully planned one—brings. Ultimately, you want to reach your goals without getting lost along the way. The process of Life Mapping offers you a way to take inventory of your life. Not the *things* in your life; your very *life*. It gives you the opportunity to reflect on and commit to the things that are really important to you during your stay on this earth. And it challenges you to find ways to manifest those things *now* while the opportunity is present. Life Mapping is a tool to help you find your way.

The Paradox of Planning

You can plan your life. And yet you can't. That is the basic paradox behind the premise of Life Mapping. In fact, the entire process is like life, paradoxical—simple yet complex, requiring us to look without and within. When you engage in this process, you are embracing the control you have over the uncontrollable, and you are accepting that the uncontrollable will always be present.

Part of the contradiction of life is that we are not in charge of very much, yet the universal law of attraction (which we'll explore more, later) says we can determine or influence everything about our lives. Even if you don't believe in God or some higher power, you have to acknowledge that things happen to you over which you have absolutely no control—you'll be laid off, your spouse will die, your child will be born with a birth defect, you'll contract some serious disease. Or you'll turn the corner and bump into the person who turns out to be the love of your life.

Most people also believe that human beings have freedom of choice and that this freedom gives us the opportunity to influence the things that happen in our lives. It is this paradox that supports and confuses us simultaneously. But if we explore and examine this seeming contradiction—as we will in these pages—we can hold both of these conflicting realities in our hearts and minds. They are not mutually opposed.

Thus, you do have the ability to create your reality *and* there is a higher power that influences what happens in the world. That power has a plan that makes sense of things that appear senseless. Part of this truth lies in the fact that there is so much that you can't see and don't know that is influencing your world. Ultimately that makes you, and us, riders on the road of life. (Even if you stubbornly stand still and refuse to move or change; the weather, the shifts in topography, or the Department of Transportation will change the road and you will have to respond to that one way or another.)

Life Mapping helps you navigate the road's bends and bumps and gives you an appreciation of the tools you already possess to make the journey, much like the Orienteer with their compass and map.

I now invite you to begin this new phase of your journey with awareness and purpose through the process of Life Mapping.

Coming to Terms

Now, before we move too far along into the process and principles of Life Mapping, there are some terms and concepts that are important. Each concept is defined here and will be used and discussed in more depth throughout the book.

PURPOSE:

Your "purpose" is the reason you're on the planet. It intimidates some people to speak of life's purpose because it sounds like some big, deep thing—pages and pages of a grand manifesto, something detailed and dissected and written in stone. In fact, your purpose on the planet may be simply to comfort people or to learn unconditional love or to influence someone's life. Everyone is here to do something and to receive something. Purpose is what you and the Universe agreed that you would do with your life. The more you seek it, the more it will be revealed. Life Mapping is about finding your purpose for being, then moving with that.

MISSION:

Your mission is how you will accomplish your purpose. Sometimes there is confusion between mission and purpose. They are similar, yet there is a distinction that is important. If purpose is what you want or need to do, then, mission is how you plan to do it. It's your intentional movement toward the manifestation of your desires.

Purpose is the end; mission is the means. For example, if your purpose is to help save lives, you could do this by becoming a doctor, a teacher, an inventor, a change-management consultant, a mother or a missionary. The "how" is the fulfillment of your heart's desire, the use of your gifts to make the difference you are destined to make. This allows for complete success and happiness because by doing what you love, you provide the world with what the Universe needs from you.

It's important to know that your personal mission may have very little to do with how you make a living and everything to do with how you live. Your hobbies, volunteer work, and child-rearing are often the fulfillment of your purpose here on this earth. A dear friend and mother of two beautiful children once told me: "I'm done." She felt that she had brought these two spiritual beings into this world and if she did nothing else in life, she had made a huge contribution and fulfilled her purpose in life.

VALUES:

Values are those ideas and core beliefs that you consciously and unconsciously live by–the ideals that influence how you make hard choices, guide your desires and priorities, inform your decision-making and are embedded in your actions. Values are both supportive and limiting; they are a choice, and sometimes the impact of our values-based decisions is unintentional and unexpected.

Some people would have us believe that only certain values are acceptable. Others use values to manipulate people to do things like a good marketing strategy uses sex to make you buy that car that you don't need or buy a certain brand of beer with the assumption that a beautiful girl will be attracted to you if she sees you drinking a particular beverage. Exercises in later chapters will help you discover your true values, and you will be able to see clearly how they are working in your life and whether they serve you well or not so well. When you take time to examine your values closely, you open your heart and mind to other ideas or beliefs that may serve you better.

VISION:

Vision is your picture of your ideal state—how you see life and what you believe is possible. We move towards the pictures we create. When you create your own picture of the future, you are better able to create your future versus the future that other people are creating for you with their own pictures. Life Mapping asks that you create a vision of your ideal lifestyle and discern what is required for you to have it. Using the tools in this book, you can define and articulate the things you desire, creating a vivid picture of the end result. That, in turn, will help you make choices that advance and further clarify your vision, mission, and purpose.

MANIFESTATION:

The physical or tangible result of your visions and actions is the manifestation. When you manifest your vision, you bring it into existence, you make it real. This is the result of all of the concepts described above.

STRATEGIC ACTION:

Strategic actions are the key steps needed to deal with blocks that would keep you from moving forward toward your vision. We all have blocks. If we didn't, we would be living our ideal life now. Thinking strategically involves looking at the big picture and all the little details—past, present and future—while scanning the environment all the time for the 'best' route, the best actions. It means previewing the consequences of your various choices before you make them. Ideally, you will be able to make decisions that allow a single action to take you ten giant steps forward, as opposed to one or two baby steps toward your vision. It's not just taking action but taking essential or critical actions—purposefully.

COMMITMENT:

The backbone of vision is commitment because it describes your devotion to your own goal. When you make a true commitment, you are joining your own vision with the greater energy of the Universe, so that you are moving in synchronicity with that Power on your chosen path. When that happens, you enter the realm of what people like to call coincidence.

Commitment allows what people call Providence to move, making room for all kinds of miracles to take place to bring you exactly what you need in the moment. Like when you forget your wallet and have to go back to the house, which allows you to catch the phone call that gives you the information you need to have before you go into the meeting you were headed for before you realized you didn't have your wallet. I can't explain how it happens; I only know that when it happens to me, I feel like I'm walking through a movie. And I know that when faith and commitment come together with vision, you will know (and stay on) the right path—the one that will help you reach your destination, even if you can't explain it to anyone else.

Now that we have some common definitions for these terms, we can get started. Your understanding of these concepts will support you in laying the foundation for creating your Life Map. These terms will be referred to throughout the book. This book is designed to be a workbook. The exercises will support you in building your Life Map and understanding not only where you want to go but where you are and what is getting in the way of your living your ideal lifestyle.

Getting Your Bearings

Before you get on the road, it's best to know where you are going. The good news is that, as I said in the introduction, "all answers lie within." The challenge is getting to the answers. Unfortunately, we are so bombarded by words, ideas, information, misinformation, noise, advertising, propaganda, institutional rhetoric, and other people telling us that what we want is impossible, wrong, selfish, or bad; that we get confused about what our wants, desires, and needs truly are. We forget what we know about ourselves and about others.

The first step toward remembering is to listen deeply. To do that, you must get to a silent place where there is no noise, no voices, no words—and *stay there* until your real truth is revealed. At first, this can be a scary place to be—sitting deep within you. But if you keep sitting long enough, you'll realize that there is no one there but you and your spirit. Nothing frightening is there at all. Eventually, you will become comfortable and comforted in this space. I've found that, after some practice, I'm now very much in touch with what is real for me—and, if I'm ever uncertain, I know that the process of sitting in silence is a sure way to find out if something holds true for me.

Some people call this prayer; some, meditation; others have other names for seeking wisdom within. Call it whatever has meaning for you. But put it into practice. I can tell you that when I can't seem to find the right information or when I am confused about what or where or how—going inward is a good place for me to find direction.

Direction may come in different forms. Sometimes you may be directed to seek help. A question may come to you and you may be directed to ask a certain person this question. It could be that you realize that you are wasting your time doing something and need to redirect your energy toward something else that will move your vision forward. It may sound as quiet as a whisper or be a feeling whose meaning becomes clear. You may realize that you no longer need to be involved in a relationship that you thought you could not live without. The answer you get may not come in the form or shape that you expect. Being open is key.

Then, once the information is revealed to you, you have choices. You can choose to receive it or not. You can choose to act on it or not. But having the information you need is a crucial step toward creating your Life Map.

Try This

Meditation is the simple act of quieting your mind. Moving lovingly away from the mind-chatter of your constant thoughts, releasing the noise of the environment, of your devices, allows you to connect to your spirit and inner knowing. So try it.

If you are new to meditation, here are a few options:

1. Simply sit somewhere comfortable without radio, TV or other outside noise for 5-15 minutes; just pay attention to your breathing and when thoughts appear, gently move back to focusing on your breath. See how you feel.
2. Dance without music for 10-15 minutes, move how your spirit needs you to move;
3. Walk with the intention of quieting your mind for 10-15;

When I started, moving was the key. I made everyday chores a medication. So, Enjoy and find peace.

Getting the most from the process

We all learn in different ways. Some of us need to read about a thing in order to grasp it; others prefer to see a live demonstration. You may be the kind of person who has to experience it for yourself before a concept to makes sense. And, when we're talking about learning to change long-time habits or ways of thinking—which is exactly what we're doing with Life Mapping—it may mean you have to use multiple learning techniques in order to make the new understanding stick. This isn't as simple as putting tab A in slot B. We're talking about changing your life, your mind, your heart, maybe even your beliefs. That's no small task. For this reason, I've included different types of information and exercises for you to try. In this book, you'll find essays and stories, exercises, meditations, and affirmations.

The essays and stories will be most useful if you spend some time thinking about how the story or subject matter relates and doesn't relate to you and your journey. It might challenge you or give you some new perspective on your present and past experiences. Look for the lesson that the story offers you.

Exercises, included in each chapter, are designed to assist you in creating your own life map. I will often ask you to write about a subject because it can help you focus your thoughts, it becomes a record that you can read again, and it's physical—the act of moving your hand as you think about something helps ingrain it into your mind. Journaling is a great tool to capture the thoughts, questions, ideas and life experiences that come to mind as you read this book and do the exercises. Often, journaling exercises will be combined with other kinds of exercises from various chapters. Take advantage of them.

If you choose not to use writing as the tool for focusing and revisiting your thoughts, find some way of documenting your process. Drawing or some other creative means of expressing what comes to mind or talking into a recording device, the intent is to document your thoughts in a way that you can go back and look at it later.

Whatever method you choose to document your ideas, it is important that you spend time in silence focusing on the tasks of the exercise. (I can't stress enough the value of spending quiet, concentrated time doing these exercises where there are no distractions.) In order to get the best from the exercises, you need to really give some thought to what you are writing. If you only give short, off the cuff, or perfunctory answers to the exercises or if you don't give the exercises the concentrated thought suggested, you won't reap all the benefits and clarity that is possible from this process.

Meditations and affirmations are ways to strengthen ideas and concepts that may take a while for you to fully digest understand and implement into daily actions. They are included to help you move through the work of self-discovery by offering practice and time for reflection about the concepts and ideas explored in the chapter essays and stories. Try affirmations for several days or weeks. I find that 30-90 days is a good amount of time to feel the full effects of most affirmations. See how it feels.

I began saying an affirmation each morning to assist me with my thinking about abundance – having more than enough. After a few weeks, I noticed that I wasn't running on empty all the time. As I kept using the affirmation, I began to have enough to pay my bills on time and in full. My resources continued to increase. By the end of the second year, I had quadrupled my income. I am convinced that in addition to all of the groundwork that I had been doing for years, the affirmation helped me to make those final shifts that allowed me to attract the prosperity that I was seeking.

Again, use journaling to document how your own thinking is affected by using affirmations. If it feels useful, you may want to create affirmations for different aspects of your life. Keep them short and easy to repeat, write them down and tuck them into your pocket or purse, or post them on your fridge, bulletin board or dashboard.

Even after you've used these tools to create your Life Map, you can always go back to them when you come up against issues or obstacles later.

That's a lot, to begin with—but it gets even richer as you continue the process. Now that we're on the same page with regard to the premise of Life Mapping and the concepts and ideas we'll be working with, let's get busy.

CHAPTER 2: VISION-SEEING THE UNSEEN

We move towards the pictures we create.

Internationally respected leadership authority, family expert and organizational consultant, Steven Covey says, "Start with the end in mind." In order to create a map to your ideal future, you need to know where you want to end up. In this chapter, we'll work on creating a vision of your ideal future.

Every successful entrepreneur, inventor or creator started with an idea that only they could see a vision no one else had. They were able to imagine what was not yet possible—and held that vision firmly until it was no longer a vision but had manifested in reality. And that's the goal, isn't it? To manifest our own magnificent, creative ideas? That's certainly the goal of Life Mapping—and one of the most important gifts of Life Mapping is **vision**.

Some people are naturally visionary; for others of us, developing a clear vision takes some effort. And everyone faces the task of holding on to a vision in the face of critique, ridicule, lack of support, too much support, or other obstacles. The clearer your vision is, however, and the more completely thought out, the easier it is to hold on to it.

Freeing your mind

To prepare for creating your vision, it's helpful to start by reaching back to a time of innocence in your life, when everything seemed possible. A time when your impression of your abilities enabled you to say things like, "I want to be a professional football player and, in the off-season, I will be a brain surgeon"—and to believe that was possible.

You may have to go back quite a way to get to that place. Your vision may come into conflict with the way you're "supposed" to think. As a child, daydreaming was a wondrous, magical time of exploring what I could not explore in real life. My teachers and other adults, however, considered my daydreaming was a time-waster, an indulgence in unrealistic fantasies when I should have my mind on the matters at hand. They meant well; they wanted to steer me in the 'right' direction and help me to be practical.

Often, those who love and care about us inadvertently limit us based on their own fears. They discourage our dreaming and encourage us to see only the "reality" that is in front of us. But your ability to dream resides in that place within you where your thoughts were totally free of the baggage that comes from listening to other people's opinions or advice—even well-intentioned people who are trying to protect you from disappointment by limiting your thinking.

For me, one of those well-intentioned people was my Dad. I wanted to be a movie star like Audrey Hepburn, Dorothy Dandridge, and Sophia Loren. He'd never actually known anyone who'd made a living as an actress. He didn't know how that would be possible. He didn't want to see me suffer or fail, so his way of protecting me was to say, "Acting is great, but why don't you major in something that you can actually make a living at?" My dream held fast, and I was not deterred. Not at first. But over time, those kinds of statements had an impact. I continued to pursue a career in the entertainment industry, but I turned my attention to the more practical side of the business—theater management.

So, I am personally very aware that some of you reading this may have forgotten how to dream and are limited in the way you think about your future. But I am just as aware that you can free your mind once again, reclaiming or reinventing your vision. In this chapter, we're going to begin to practice. The next few exercises are designed to help you go back to a place where everything seems possible, where you can think and imagine and dream without limits. Seem like a monumental task? It's not. Just let yourself relax and dream. And remember, if you don't like what you create, you can always start over and create something more to your liking.

Journaling exercise

Think back to a time when you were very young, and everything seemed possible.

- What did you want to be when you grew up?
- What did your parents, siblings, neighbors, teachers or friends say when you told them about your dream?
- What impact have those words had on your life?
- Did you pursue your dream?

Write about your thoughts and feelings about how you approached or didn't approach the dream you envisioned.

Then go outside and in a safe way, burn the paper as a way to release these limiting thoughts and the impact they have had on your thinking.

Note: safe means the papers are in a non-flammable container away from buildings or debris so they cannot catch anything else on fire. (these safety instructions are as a precaution as young people and others will read this and I want everyone to be safe.

<u>Exercise: My Ideal Day</u>

This exercise gives you a specific way to focus on the vision of your ideal lifestyle. It is designed to help you gain clarity on how you want to spend your time and what success looks like for you.

Materials:

For this exercise, you will need an open mind and a way to capture your thoughts so that you can access them later. Write them, log them into your computer, or use a tape recorder—whatever works for you.

Instructions:

Begin by sitting for a few minutes in silence. Clear away mundane thoughts and open your mind. Now, moving into a world of infinite possibilities, envision being at the pinnacle of your success—a place and position in which you are doing and being everything you want. Now, describe an ideal day from the time you wake up in the morning until you go to bed at night. Describe what you will be doing, who you'll interact with, where you'll go, what you'll wear, what you'll eat.

Be sure to include all aspects of your life—personal, business, material, social. Envision how your lifestyle is financed and see yourself receiving money or other symbols of abundance. See the day in all the detail you can imagine, and use your five senses—sight, sound, taste, touch, and smell— to describe these details.

In this process, answer the obvious questions: What do I want? How do I want to spend my time? Who do I want to spend time with? What kind of environment do I want around me? What impact do I want to have on others? Write down what you envision. Think about it. Revise it.

When I have clients in my workshops do this exercise, they often come up against feelings of limitation.

Frequently Asked Questions:

What if I can't fit everything into one day? Write one day at a time. That's the way we live. Make several days which expand on the different kinds of experiences you envision for yourself. I have done several examples of my Ideal Day.

What if I don't want to do anything like what I am doing now? Then don't. In fact, that may be the whole point for you—to realize that your ideal day is nothing like your real days, and it's time for a change. On the other hand, you may also realize that you are living aspects of your ideal life, and you may only need to make small tweaks in order to be living a near-perfect life. In any case, this is your dream time. You can do whatever you want in your dreams.

What if I just can't do it? You can do it. Start small. If tomorrow was an ideal day, what would it look, feel, taste and smell like? Then you can project out: In one month, what would your ideal day look like? In six months? In a year?

Making Meaning of Your Ideal Day

Now that you are satisfied with your ideal day, read it slowly. Take in the words and vision that you have created. Let your vision impact you intellectually, emotionally, spiritually. Think about how you will feel and experience your life when you have achieved this ideal. Savor it.

At the same time, think about the pieces of your ideal day that you can make happen immediately? Are there changes that you could make today that would lay the foundation for what you want to happen in your future? In your journal, make a list of ideas or actions that would be easy for you to implement immediately. Keep it short and simple—three to five items—and post it somewhere that you can see it several times a day.

Then make a commitment to doing each one of the things on the list—implementing it into your routine starting now. Later, I'll ask you to look at some other aspects of your ideal day. Once you know what your ideal day would look like, it's easier to start making your days more "ideal" by taking actions to manifest these ideas, little by little.

Exercise: My Retirement Party Exercise

This exercise focuses on a different aspect of your vision. It is a way for you to get in touch with what accomplishments are important for you to make, how you want people to remember you, and what kinds of relationships you want in your life. This exercise helps you look at the end result of your life's work. This exercise is about IMPACT.

Materials:

For this exercise, you will need an open mind and a way to capture your thoughts so that you can use this information later.

Part One:

Create a story about yourself. Imagine you are at an age and position in life that you have accomplished all of your dreams and desires, and you are ready to slow down, pass the torch and retire. The people who love you have planned a party honoring your life and your contributions, and all of the people you have touched in your life are present and they each take time to share their thoughts about you and what you have meant to them. Describe this event and the people present in as much detail as you can imagine. What do you want them to say? What have you accomplished that has meaning? What legacy are you leaving for the people who will follow you?

Part Two:

Now, imagine that your retirement party is today. Write a story about your retirement party based on your current reality. If your party were today -- Who would be there? What would people say about how you have touched their lives both positively and negatively? If unpleasant relationships come to mind, think about what that person might say and how you feel about it. What would you like to say to that person? What would it take to reconcile the relationship? What have you accomplished thus far in your life—both big and small? What legacy are you leaving now?

Making Meaning of Your Retirement Party

Review your retirement stories. You now have two versions of your retirement party. They are different. Your awareness is probably heightened with regards to the contrasts and similarities of the scenarios you have created. Use the reflection questions in the following box to think through this exercise. This will give you some ideas about any changes or actions you want to take in your life as a response to this exercise.

Reflection Questions – Things to Think About

Look back at both exercises and compare the answers in your ideal day, your ideal retirement and your immediate retirement. What is similar about them? What is incongruent? What excites you about these pictures? What seems doable? What makes you uncomfortable? What have you learned? What do you need to do to make your reality more like your ideal life? Make notes in your journal.

Now, add any important actions from this exercise to the list of 3-5 items you wrote in the "My Ideal Day" exercise.

Making meaning of it all

The primary question for both of these exercises is: *How do I need to "be", in order to live my ideal lifestyle and have the relationships that I want in my life?*

When I first described my ideal day ten years ago, I envisioned that I would get up early in the morning and light candles, exercise and meditate. Then I would take a shower and meet my children in the kitchen for a breakfast of fresh fruit, tea, and a healthy shake. As soon as I looked at it on paper, in black and white, I realized that I was in control of my morning and I could make that part of my ideal day a reality immediately. I began to get up an hour earlier than normal so I would have time to exercise, meditate and pray, visualize my future and/or read something inspiring. Although we still eat pancakes once in a while, I make sure that on most mornings I have fresh fruit or a fruit smoothie available for my children and myself at breakfast.

This simple change has made a huge difference in the way that I feel and, in my ability to stay focused and balanced as I juggle all the demands on my time and energy. It has reminded me that my ideal lifestyle is not limited by my checkbook balance. My happiness, my ideal lifestyle is more a state of mind translated into the quality of the life I live.

For you, allowing your awareness to grow is all that is called for. Stay in the visioning place for a little longer so you can become really clear about what you really want and how you want to live before moving to your current reality. At every turn, you have the opportunity to learn about yourself, how you think, what triggers your thoughts and actions. It is all part of discovering how to create your ideal future and this is what Life Mapping is all about.

My retirement party became a reality.

When I first did my retirement party exercise, I envisioned an elaborate party with great food, music, and all of my clients, mentees, family, etc. I really enjoyed writing the story.

In 2017, I celebrated the 30th Anniversary of my business, MKM Management Consulting. My husband and I decided to have a big BBQ and have clients, colleagues, friends, family over to celebrate and share in this pivotal moment in my business career. We set up a video camera for people to send shout outs and congratulations like you would at a wedding. In talking with the videographer, I realized I needed to make some statements. OK. That was the plan. Then when I was doing that, my Gestalt OSD Center colleagues and friends stepped up and asked to speak. At that time, they presented me with the Gestalt Organization Systems Development Center's Life-Time Achievement Award. I was a weeping mess as they really surprised me, and I was so honored and touched.

It was at that time that I realized I was living my retirement party. The people that were impactful and that I cared about were there (or sent their love) and I was hearing about the impact I had made with my life's work.

I share this because it was so impactful on me. I felt truly loved, seen and I realized that I had already made a difference with my presence and my work in the world. There is so much more for me to do, that I can envision, and it was amazing to stop and look at all that I had already done. My life's work was before me. And Life Mapping clearly had an impact on my being able to create that work, those relationships, and accomplishments. It was intentional in that I got clear about how I wanted to be in the world and what I needed to do to manifest the "retirement party" of my dreams. Now for the third act.

Again, it has been amazing to watch my vision manifest in so many ways over these years and see how I am manifesting new things with Everett. I look forward to hearing about how you are manifesting as you implement Life Mapping and lean into the journey you have mapped out.

Excerpt from My Ideal Day
8-22-98

I wake up early. The sun is just beginning to shed light on the day. My husband, sleeping warm beside me, makes me pause before I get out of bed. I resist the temptation to stay and I let my feet hit the cool wood floors of my room. I light a candle in my meditation corner that casts a warm glow in the room against the sun's impending light. I move to the French doors that lead to the balcony as I put on another layer of soft white cotton to shield me against the cool morning air. As I step out onto the balcony, the air is light and soft and cool against my face. There are large crystals sitting in the corners and a few plants hanging overhead. I see the moon and look for the sun. I begin my morning exercise ritual of tai chi and yoga then, after working up a light sweat, sit to breathe, meditate and think about what is needed from me for the day.

After about 20 minutes, I rise energized. I get my husband stirring and head for the shower. The sun is in its full morning position and it's a wonderful day. I throw on a simple cotton pantsuit and head downstairs to meet the children for breakfast. My youngest son is still in his pajamas and the oldest is dressed and eating his breakfast of fruit, cereal, and juice. I share some fruit with them and mix my morning shake. We chat excitedly about their school day and their other activities. We talk about what we will do for the weekend as my husband, now dressed for work, joins us. He kisses us all lovingly and sips tea as we make our plans. He's dressed in casual business attire and seems easy going and relaxed. I scoot the children off to school. We grown-ups finish tea and have a precious few moments alone before moving into our day.

I head to my office and check the fax and e-mail and look to see how many hits have been made to my web site. I call my associates to confirm our preparation meeting for this week's training and consulting activities. They'll come to me. My office is full of light, fairly neat and orderly. Some fresh fruit and water sit on the credenza. I begin to edit the talking outline for my next speaking engagement when my editor calls. She has reviewed the first draft of my newest book and is very pleased. She also updates me on what's happening with my book deal: the publishers are thrilled that we are delivering a draft so soon. They are also pleased that my popularity is growing on the speaker circuit because of the positive impact it should have on book sales. We take a moment to celebrate our victory. It only seems like yesterday that we had a late-night conversation about how she could help me and others in our circle write the books we had inside us. And it's working. Next month we will meet at our retreat place with all the family and have both a vacation, and work session to finish editing the book. Until then we will e-mail changes back and forth. Technology has really helped my business grow.

I smell fresh basil and garlic wafting into my office from the kitchen. My housekeeper is a great cook and a mother's helper. She helps me keep it all together on the home front, especially when I am traveling. Just as I decide I can no longer resist temptation and move towards the kitchen for a sample, the doorbell rings. My associates have arrived for lunch and our weekly planning session. They are independent consultants who are now working with me almost full time. Each of them has unique talents and skills and we all share some basic skills that allow us to supplement and substitute for each other as needed.

Usually, they are lead coordinators on the projects and then we pull each other in as needed for specific tasks. We greet each other, begin to catch up in the foyer and move into the large dining room that doubles as a conference room. It too is bright and has two blank walls which we use for wall charts. The other wall has two large windows sandwiching a beautiful piece of art. The other side of the dining room is open into the hall-atrium that connects with the great room. Light streams in from the skylights in the atrium and magnifies the energy that permeates the house–energy of peace, love, and excitement about life. I'm surrounded by my favorite colors, lots of turquoises, purples, deep greens, eggshell, and peach. It's a house of simple beauty. After lunch, we go over the updated project calendar. When we take a break, I go to my office and check my mail. A contract from a new client has arrived, with a big deposit check enclosed. Several other checks are also in today's mail–fees for training and facilitation sessions. That reminds me: I grab a handful of envelopes each with a check-in it for my associates. I have made a habit of having their fees ready at every other meeting. "Share the wealth" is a philosophy that has paid off handsomely for me. It makes me feel good too.

As we reconvene, I smile knowing that I will be able to give a little gift to colleagues I care about and who are responsible for my current business growth. We work a few hours and I send the basket around with the envelopes. I see surprised smiles from my colleagues as they peek into their envelope. You see, when I get paid, they get paid. Sometimes we have more than we expect.

I work to make sure that these meetings end about the time that the children return from their day. I say goodbye to my colleagues, and I greet my two little men as they arrive home from school. I help prepare their snack and sit down to help with homework. As they do their homework, I finish opening the mail and select something from my reading stack.

As part of this ritual, I find out about their day and what they've learned. We put the final touches on dinner. The boys help with dinner by making a salad and setting the table. As they set the table, 'Papa' arrives home from work with kisses and hugs for everyone. He had a productive day but is glad to be home with his family. I hand him his mail and he goes to his study to unwind before dinner. We have dinner as a family and a few friends join us for dessert and coffee. I help get the kids ready for bed and tuck them in before joining our company for some adult social time. About 9:30 p.m. they are saying goodbye and promising to beat us at cards soon. After we walk them out, my husband and I take advantage of this quiet time together by taking a walk in the garden. We tidy up the kitchen together before retiring. As we turn out the lights and head up the stairs, I feel two strong hands softly massage my shoulders. They have drifted down to my waist by the time I get to our bedroom. I smile. I am glad it's fairly early because I have a busy day tomorrow. I think about the luncheon I will be speaking at and the other two client meetings I will attend as I slip into bed and the arms of my lover. Then all of those thoughts fade as his smell invades my senses...

Exercise: Capturing Your Vision

The chart below gives you a simple format for capturing what is important to you about your vision. Use your thinking from the Ideal Day and Retirement Party exercises as well as what you know about yourself. List the categories that are the important areas in your life. For me, the categories were family, spiritual development, career/business, community, material possessions, and education. Write down your categories in the space at the top of each box.

> Having trouble?
>
> **Try This:**
>
> Try making a list of 10 to 15 things that you want in your future. Start small. I want more time to.... I want to experience.... I want to have.... I have always wanted to.... See how these things overlap or fall into categories. If you get stuck, draw a blank, reflect on what would happen if you declared your want and you got it.

Now, fill in the boxes with three to five of the most important ideas that you want to bring to fruition as part of your ideal lifestyle. If your ideal lifestyle includes happy children who are successful in their careers, put that under family. If you had a positive fulfilling and loving relationship with your significant other, list that. My "material" list included a really nice house; since then I have added a full-length silver fox fur coat.

Vision

Congratulations! You have created your vision for your ideal lifestyle. Now, you get to find things you can do each moment of each day to manifest this vision. Now that you have written this, the Universe is moving to support you in making this vision real.

Making Your Vision Real

Visioning is about dreaming. Life Mapping is about finding a path to make those dreams real in this lifetime. It is also about finding ways to enjoy the journey by appreciating where you are and how perfectly your present circumstances support your vision. Many times, we think that we are in the wrong place, but I have learned over time that I am always in just the right place based on what I am willing to accept in my life. When I am willing and ready for a new aspect of my dream to come true, it does, sometimes instantly.

The first task in developing vision is remembering how to dream. You have done this. The next step is controlling your thinking and behavior so you can turn those dreams into reality.

<u>Something to think about.</u>

Dreaming is one way to discover your gifts and get in touch with your heart's desires. What do you love doing? What would you love doing every day even if you didn't get paid for it?

Knowing what you want

Ultimately, deep down, we all know what we want. But sometimes it is hard for us to admit what we really want. If you find yourself saying, "I don't know what I want," I suggest you explore what is getting in the way of your declaring what you *do* want. Often times we get stuck in some form of fear that keeps us from accepting what we want. I once worked with a woman who wanted to be a dancer. Wendy was very talented, but she didn't have the body type that the industry required. She soon realized that she was missing the window of opportunity to be a professional dancer. She married and had children.

In her second career, she became a dance teacher. She has spent the last ten years encouraging inner-city kids to pursue their dreams in the arts and giving them the beginning tools to do just that. She loves her work. Wendy is living her dream in a different way than she envisioned and is having more impact than she ever thought possible. She is my best friend and I am so proud of her.

The other side of this story has to do with all the things that got in this beautiful and powerful woman's way and what it took for her to overcome all the judgment from others so that she could realize that she was living her dream even if it didn't match what others thought she ought to be doing. This is a layered process. It requires a desire to move forward and a willingness to look honestly at your current circumstances without judgment and without rose-colored glasses. In the next chapter, I will share some insights and exercises to help you move through the blocks to your vision.

Be Encouraged

You are doing great! Take time at each turn on this Journey to allow the insights and inner knowing to take hold in your spirit. Then keep moving through the process at your own pace.

Enjoying the Scenery

In addition to knowing where you want to be at the end of your journey, it is equally important to paint a picture of the experience you want to have during the journey. Some like to take the quickest route; others the scenic route. Some people must take the most economical means of transportation. Others travel first class. While you are planning your journey, you must also look at what it will take to create the experience you want to have while you're en route to your destination.

After all, this is your life we're talking about, not a week-long trip to Disneyworld. You are going to be moving in the direction of your vision every day for the rest of your life. You don't want to be so focused on getting "there" that you don't enjoy the sights along the way. That is part of Life Mapping—creating a way to enjoy your whole life and finding ways to achieve balance in all aspects of your life, to connect to those you love and to do what you love in meaningful ways. All this has to be put consciously onto your map. I have asked you to take time to explore what you want so that when it's time to figure out how you will get it, you will be working from a full picture of the life and lifestyle you want to lead and the values that will shape how you get there. These things are part of the journey—as important a part as the destination itself.

Chapter 3: Current Reality Where Are You Now?

All judgment is self-judgment.

Determining where you are right now in relation to where you want to be is the next step in Life Mapping. Your current reality is the starting place for understanding what you need to do now and what you need to do next. Neither Map Quest nor AAA can give you directions to your destination without knowing your starting location. The same concept holds true for Life Mapping: in order to move forward, you have to be clear about where you are. When you are able to state what is true in this moment, you can see more clearly where you are and begin to chart a path towards your next destination.

One friend calls this aspect of the process the "get a grip and get real" part. It's time to make the shift from the dream world where we mentally create the things we want to see ourselves doing, and move to the concrete and tangible aspects of your life—the nitty-gritty reality of now.

In this chapter, I am asking you to shed the rose-colored-glasses (though they are an important and necessary part of the process) and start looking at your current reality in a factually and non-judgmentally way. This chapter will help you increase your awareness of your situation and what you want. It is another step toward looking at what is getting in the way of your living your vision and loving your life.

I can imagine that some of you will be sighing with relief: *Ah, finally, we can deal with something concrete!"* Others of you will feel nervous or challenged by the need to leave the visions and deal with the nitty-gritty. Your reaction will be based on your preferred style of processing information. Don't hold any judgment about which place is better, or more practical. They are both necessary steps in mapping your future.

Stating what "is" will raise your awareness of your current situation in ways that might surprise you. At least once a year, as I look at my life map, I update my current reality to account for how my life has evolved and changed and to rejoice in how much closer I am to my vision and my ideal lifestyle. I am always surprised at how much I have accomplished. I have often discovered important new things that I had not paid attention to before. Going through this process gives me a moment to celebrate before the goal-oriented part of me reminds me of the long list of things that are still to be accomplished. And I find myself grateful for the balance.

What's Real, What's Now

In Life Mapping, when we talk about "current reality," we mean just that. It's a fact-based statement about your real, in-this-moment situation. Your current reality is a description of your current situation, your strengths, assets, liabilities, challenges, obstacles, and opportunities. It's everything that is going on in your life that can have an impact on where you want to go. It's about taking a picture of where you are.

Unfortunately, one of the things we have trouble with is accurately and objectively assessing where we are, what we are actually doing, how efficiently we're moving. The difficulty lies in looking at our behavior and our actions without judgment. Everything we have learned and experienced has taught us to assess something along a continuum of bad to good. So, when we look at our current status, we tend to place that kind of judgment on it. But reality has nothing to do with our perception or experience. It is simply data, facts, points on the map along the journey.

For example, when you are traveling, there are certain facts related to your trip. If you were just stating the facts, you might say, "I started in DC, went through Baltimore, and into Philadelphia. I got lost trying to get on the New Jersey Turnpike. There was an accident at exit 9 and all the traffic had to be detoured along surface roads for two exits. I am unlikely to get to New York until after midnight."

Those are the *facts*. But that's probably not what you're *feeling*. If you look at the situation with any kind of judgment—positive or negative—your description of the trip might be something like this, "I hate going through DC; the traffic is always terrible. But I like big cities like Baltimore and Philadelphia because there's something fun to do and the food is great. I can't believe these careless drivers! Why can't people here drive like they know what they're doing? Now I'll be late getting into New York. I'm so stupid for not leaving earlier…"

In the latter case, you're not just stating facts; but you are coloring them with your fatigue or irritation from having to travel by car. Maybe you've had experiences in the cities you're passing through that influence your perception of them. If you love crab cakes and boats, you may think Baltimore is a great place to be. Or perhaps you get irritated with yourself when you're late because it was a pet peeve that your mother always complained about.

The point is, from the time we're born, we begin to understand things based on our experiences. And we register our experiences and our interpretations of them in the back of our mind—experience by experience—throughout our lives. By the time we become adults, we have a whole, complex set of beliefs by which we judge just about everything we do. Reality gets buried under there somewhere. Things that color our reality include telling polite lies, telling the naked truth, overlooking our blind spots and failing to hear and use feedback.

Try this - Judge Ye Not

Pick an object, any object. Then begin to describe it without using any words that live on the bad to good judgment continuum. Just offer the facts about the object. Write it down or have someone listen to you. This can be especially helpful if you pick something you have strong positive or negative feelings about

Polite Lies

We often delude ourselves about our current reality because we begin to believe the polite lies we tell others. When my checkbook bottoms out, I don't tell the truth when people ask, "How are you?" or "How is business?" I assume they don't want to hear the unvarnished truth, first of all. And I don't want to risk having them judge me as less successful, or less together. So, I give a half-truth, the socially correct answer, such as "Things are a little slow" or "I can always use more business." We tell people that work is going great when we're really petrified that we'll be fired before the next performance review. We put on the charade of being happily in love, when in fact we're fighting bitterly with our partner. We say we feel fine, ignoring that nagging cough that won't go away.

But it's not only about putting on a public face—which is sometimes necessary and appropriate. (You probably do need to put off the next fight with your husband until *after* the family Christmas dinner. And you don't need to be bawling about your personal issues at work.) There is a time and place for the public persona. Your problems arise when you wear the mask so often that you start to believe it. Or if you've done it for so long that you can no longer recognize the real you or the reality of your situation. I always tell my children that, "Sometimes, you may choose to lie to others but never lie to me or to yourself."

The Naked Truth

What could be wrong with telling the truth? And what could be simpler? Just state the facts, ma'am. In fact, truth-telling is an art and a skill. I admit it's one that I didn't always have. As a young person, I was bent on always telling the naked truth. I was blunt almost to the point of being disrespectful, or at least to the point of making other people uncomfortable because my truth was full of judgment. I had not learned the subtle art of truth-telling—to tell my truth "with clothing on."

The polite truth is not about sugar-coating a falsehood, or even sugar-coating the truth. (The former is still lying; the latter is flattery.) It comes from a place of compassion and respect—from a heartfelt place that enables you to give other people (and yourself!) the benefit of the doubt.

The polite truth takes into consideration that life is complex and that assessing, and judging based on what we see, will always give us an incomplete picture of what is really happening since we can never have all the information needed to understand someone else's life. The polite truth is forgiving without making excuses. It is kind and positive while saying what needs to be said. It leaves open the possibility of change. It is encouraging yet realistic.

It is saying you have a gift for seeing the challenges in a situation versus saying you always look at the negative. It is saying to the child that is acting out, what could you do to get my positive attention versus scolding them and assuming they are acting out just to get on your last nerve. It's having the difficult conversation with your co-worker from an asset-based approach by saying what is working and then what could be better or improved. It is simply a choice.

When I approach these conversations, I tend to make joining statements then differentiating statements. Once with a client, I was working to help him articulate what was needed for him to be satisfied with our services. I said, "I want you to be totally satisfied and be able to move forward with implementing this plan. I know we have different styles. I tend to be very brief and look to keep documents short because, in my experience, people don't really read long documents. And your last plan was fairly lengthy. It is just a choice; you know what will work for you and your organization. What do I need to do to support you in feeling like you are getting everything you need to move forward?" It turns out that it wasn't the document; it was that he didn't really know how to move forward, in terms of the next steps. By owning my own style in a very non-judgmental way, the client was more comfortable in owning his part of the interaction. He could have easily moved into criticizing the work, the format and not have articulated his real need so I could address it.

Feedback

We get feedback in all kinds of ways. Every time we say or do something, we have an expectation of the result. We get the action or reaction from others or ourselves. It either matches our intention and expectation or it doesn't. That information is feedback. Some feedback is verbal. A shopper complains to the store manager (direct) or simply does not come back to the store (indirect) or worse yet, the shopper starts a blog, launching a campaign to convince others to stop shopping there. Some feedback is physically observable data or phenomenological. You have conversations every day with people and notice their phenomenological reactions.

They swallow hard, their brow wrinkles, they smile or laugh, they cry, their eyes look down. Some feedback is energetic. You just feel the vibe or the energy of the situation. You get data in all sorts of ways. Some feedback feels positive and affirming. Some feedback feels negative because it triggers a judgment or experience from our past that hurts or scares us or puts us on the defensive.

I find that the most powerful kind of feedback is often unsolicited. It happens when someone offers me honest observations about some aspect of myself that was not in my awareness. They make me aware of my blind spot. There was a period of time when I was really going through a lot of heartaches. I was in a personal growth group and really struggling. The feedback I kept getting was that I looked like a goddess, I was so beautiful. This was so far away from where I was inside myself; I blew it off at first. It was difficult for me to think that anyone would find me beautiful or goddess-like. But over time, I began to see what they were paying attention to. I realized that I was powerful and beautiful even though I saw every flaw I had; others did not experience me that way. I began to practice what my grandmother had advised years ago. "Just say thank you".

Feedback is difficult to accept even when it's good. So, when the feedback is something we don't want to hear, our defenses go up even higher. We diminish it, deny it, and refuse to believe it. Sometimes we let ourselves believe it when we know it is not true. For example, the girl who thinks she is ugly because some boy that she had a crush on in grade school teased her in front of the other boys in her class. Or the words of a parent or teacher that cut like a knife when unconsciously delivered.

When it's constructively given by an informed, respected source—and when it is heard without defensiveness—feedback is very useful information. We can use it to determine whether our actions match our intentions, whether we are coming across as we think we are, to determine where we are performing above par and where we can use some improvement. And it takes practice. With practice, you can choose to find something useful in negative or hurtful feedback. A spouse's angry comment that starts with "you always" or "you never" – fill in the blank. Although it may not be true that you never do that, you can remind yourself that they experience you as not doing it. It is up to you to begin to explore alone or with that person what is creating that experience for them by stating your intention and hearing the impact that your actions are having on them. This usually happens when your intention does not match the impact or when something is so out of your awareness that you feel blindsided by the feedback. With practice, you can begin to look beyond each person's emotional effect and look deeper to see what is needed.

One client's boss was on the verge of firing her because of her attitude. It turned out that they were both misinterpreting each other's actions without checking out the assumptions they were making. He felt she was not getting the work done because she was being too social. She felt disrespected by his need to know where she was and what she was doing at all times. Over time she began to look at the situation from his point of view and see what his needs might be and explore the situation from his perspective. Her attitude changed and as her interactions began to shift from a defensive posture to one that supported his needs, their entire work relationship began to change. They began to rebuild the trust needed for them to work effectively together. By checking out their assumptions about each other or the stories they were making up about each other's behavior and actions, they began to see the "what is" without the judgment and defensiveness. They began to see each other as more human.

Saying one thing, doing another

My father used to tell me almost daily during my teens, "Your actions speak so loudly that I cannot hear your words." I would say I wanted him to trust me and yet I was sneaking around doing the very thing he'd said don't do. I was very headstrong and stubborn. But I couldn't see how my actions contradicted my words because I was so intent on being right and having him understand my intentions. I have a girlfriend who had been in an abusive relationship. She would call and talk to me about what had happened. So often her boyfriend would say he loved her and that he wanted a family, but he spent most of his time out in the street. He was loving around his friends but at home, he was totally unconcerned about her well-being. I found myself speaking my father's words to her on more than one occasion as she paid more attention to his words and very little attention to his actions that were in direct contradiction to his words. He says he loves you and he hit's you. He says he's sorry and he hits you. You get the idea.

It is very important to look at our actions and the patterns of those actions. Good or bad. Our words can be very deceiving—especially to ourselves. For better or for worse, other people tend to see past our words and judge us based on what we do. And ultimately, what you actually do is all you have to show for your life. Anyone can talk a good game, but words disappear and are forgotten. It is the action that has a lasting impact. Seeing clearly how our actions contradict the story we tell is an important source of information that can help us move past our illusions and fantasies to a reality that we can build on.

For example, a friend of mine often talked about wanting to go to college and get a degree—and his desire seemed to become more urgent after he had children. But his actions did not match his words. He'd take a course at a community college, but he wouldn't study or do assignments. When his wife suggested that he work part-time so he could go to school, he made excuses. When he had a job that would allow him to take classes and receive tuition reimbursement, he didn't take advantage of it.

These aren't judgments, but just the facts based on his actions. He had an honorable intention—to be a good role model for his children—and he thought this was the way to do it. But he really didn't have enough interest in college to motivate him to actually apply himself. If he was being honest with himself, he might not have spent so much time talking about college but would have looked for other ways to be a good role model.

As we stop judging ourselves and creating illusions about ourselves, we can better articulate our current reality and see where we might be blinded by things not in our awareness.

Exercise: My Current Reality

Use the same categories that you created for your vision. List three to five statements about your current reality. They should be as factual as possible, describing where you are *right now* regarding these areas. Don't be too harsh with yourself. Don't beat yourself up with those "I should have..." or "what I need to do is..."

Stay away from judging your situation as bad or good. Simply state what your situation is now as factually and simply as possible.

For example: *Right now, I have $1000 in my bank account. Right now, my children are ages 10 and 12. Right now, I work doing accounting. Right now, I am divorced. Right now, I rent an apartment. Right now, I am exercising, and I am 25 pounds overweight. Right now, I have two more classes before I finish my master's degree. Right now, it will take me two more semesters to finish those classes...* You get the picture.

My Current Reality

Exercise: SWOT

Strengths, Weaknesses, Opportunities, and Threats

The SWOT exercise requires you to use the vision and current reality work you have done so far to assess your personal strengths and weaknesses. You'll assess your environment and anticipate potential opportunities that could be helpful in achieving your vision. You'll also examine potential threats and obstacles to your vision. Draw on all of the insights and awareness you have gotten from the previous exercises. SWOT is a well-used process to analyze your current situation and discern the focus of potential strategies for moving forward. Use this exercise to describe your current reality more fully. Later, this will facilitate your thinking about direction and strategy.

Think about the following questions and write your answers in the chart below.

- What are your internal strengths? Weaknesses?
- In your environment, what opportunities can you see?
- What are some potential threats to the manifestation of your vision?

Strengths	Opportunities

Weaknesses	Threats

Look over your list. What do you think are the three most important items on this chart that need to be considered as you move forward? Circle them.

Now, think about what it would take for you to maximize the positive or minimize the negative impact of the three items you circled. Write down the actions that come to mind.

The SWOT exercise is a more strategic way of looking at your internal landscape and your external environment. It will help you to prioritize and maximize what you want to work on first. If doing this exercise has given you new insights about your current reality, feel free to make any needed revisions, but resist making changes to your vision based on some perceived obstacle or threat. Potential threats and obstacles are like road construction, they require that you take this into consideration and move with caution. They sometimes require a detour. They don't have to keep you from your destination.

<u>Something to think about</u>

What is similar and/or different about the two pictures created through the Vision and the Current Reality exercises? You might look at your current reality and realize that you are living some of your vision right now. You might see that your true interests aren't really in alignment with your goal(s).

Chapter 4: Free Your Mind – Removing the Blocks to Your Vision

The Universe does not understand 'not'.

About fifteen years ago, my first husband and I found ourselves in a period where we were constantly facing financial challenges, sometimes barely able to pay the bills. We were making every effort to remedy the situation, doing without things that we needed and wanted in order to make ends meet or at least have the ends see each other. We spent a lot of effort negotiating and renegotiating who would be responsible for which bills, yet someone was always coming up short. And any time there was an emergency—say, a car in need of repair or the washing machine breaking—we found ourselves depleting the savings we had managed to put aside.

Needless to say, we argued about money a lot. I thought he should work more, get that second job that he was always talking about, be more frugal and cut back on his leisure spending. I am sure he had a list of things he thought I ought to be doing differently, too. But we couldn't hear each other, and the situation was not getting any better.

Then one day, I was lamenting to my best friend that I was concerned about being able to partner with my husband to increase our income. She said in a very matter-of-fact way, "Monika, you have the ability to make more money. What are you waiting for? Just do it. Then you can just pay the bills and let him do what he does."

It was such a simple statement, yet I had a lot of *but's: But the man 'should'... But a couple 'should'...*

As open-minded and enlightened as I thought was, I was caught between at least two outdated partnership paradigms from different decades—and neither one was working for me. I had been told all of my life that the man should provide for the family, whatever it took. My own father took various jobs—on the railroad, at a nonprofit, as a community action agency executive, as a municipal employee—to provide for us. But having grown up in the 70s, I also had strong ideas about being independent, taking care of myself, not needing anyone. My mother always told me to have my own money and never be dependent on a man. And then I had an image of marriage created in the movie studios. For the most part, I knew that wasn't real because I didn't know anyone that lived that way, yet I still wanted a version of the ideal married life created by Hollywood.

I wasn't alone. Most women and many men are caught up in the messages they learned from movies, the media, parents, books, church doctrine, political doctrine, etc. which portrays images of how life 'should' be that often have nothing to do with our own reality or our own relationships. Meanwhile, the world—economics, gender roles, marriage patterns—has changed dramatically and neither the kind of life my mother and father had, nor do the TV-manufactured marriages the likes of Dick Van Dyke and Mary Tyler Moore exist anymore.

I continued to blame my husband while I considered, reluctantly, resentfully, this idea that I was going to have to save the day by creating the resources we needed. And we all know that if you keep doing what you always do, you will keep getting what you always got. I wasn't going to get anywhere thinking the way I'd always thought.

That's what happens sometimes to our dreams and visions—they're blocked by our own limited thinking. We see things one way, which means we can't envision all the other possible ways things could be. Oh, we can see that *other* people can enjoy success in life, career, vocation, relationship or whatever, but we tell ourselves that that's not an option for us. We think that person is succeeding by some special luck, talent or miracle of birth that we weren't blessed with.

In order to manifest a vision, a dream, a goal, we have to be able to remove the mental and emotional blocks to that vision. I define blocks differently than obstacles. Obstacles are external barriers or impediments, often things we have no control over. (We will say more about those later.) Blocks, as I define them, are primarily internal challenges—something that's going on inside yourself that's hindering your own progress. Your blocks may come from your belief systems or attachments you've formed. They may be rooted in words you repeat to yourself, deep-seated beliefs, values, emotional hurts, and the way you make meaning of or interpret your experiences. Whatever the source, blocks are forms of stagnation impeding your progress toward your vision.

This chapter will help you uncover your own blocks and blind spots. It's an important step because, in order to make a Life Map—much less travel any road on that map—you have to be able to envision a way to cross the rivers, traverse the mountains, and navigate the valleys. You have to see beyond the things that seem to be blocking you.

Let's take a look at some of the common internal blocks, examine the origins of them and work on ways to recognize and remove them—or at least learn how to get around them.

What's your story?

"Tell me a story," children beg their parents and grandparents. And loving parents dutifully tell them fairy tales and legends and myths from their favorite storybooks. But we also, from the youngest age, absorb different kinds of tales and legends—things that we've been told or that we've overheard, things we have misunderstood or understood all too well. These stories are as etched in our minds as clearly as Humpty Dumpty's tragic fall or Sleeping Beauty being awakened by the handsome prince.

One example is "Don't talk to strangers"—a warning almost every child hears. "Strangers are dangerous," we tell him with the intention of keeping him safe. But think about it: Everyone outside that child's immediate family is technically a stranger, yet not all of those people are a threat. In fact, most won't be. On the other hand, 70 to 90 percent of children who are abducted or sexually abused are victims of a family member or person they know. In fact, studies also show that most children don't know what a stranger is.

In this case—and it's often the case--the story we tell is different from the complex reality in which we live—and it affects the way we deal with that reality. So, for example, if children come to deeply believe the "stranger-danger" story and become afraid of interacting with new people, it can become a block. *Maybe* it will keep them safe, but without talking to strangers, they cannot make new friends or meet people who may be put in their path to be a helpmate or a partner. Without talking to strangers, they can't ask for help or the things they need. They cannot be successful.

That's only one example of the kind of story we learn—whether we're taught deliberately, learn by osmosis or conclude based on available information or misinformation. Some of the statements that I have heard and absorbed in my lifetime include:

- It takes hard work to get anything in life
- All work and no play makes Monika a dull girl
- No one is perfect
- You can always do more (do it better)

- You have to wait for what you want
- You have to make it happen
- Pretty is what pretty does
- Work on your insides; the outside will follow
- Thin is in; fat get back
- You can do anything you put your mind to
- You can't have it all
- Powerful women are bitches
- If you are spiritual, money isn't important
- Education is the key to success

And the list goes on....

I have spent a lot of time looking at how these statements have served me and how they have gotten in my way. Many of these statements have created my work ethic, my drive for excellence, and my thirst for success. Some have served me well in creating my company and making me more visionary. Other statements have undermined my confidence and challenged my ability to accept my own power, presence, and success. They have also created in me impatience, anxiety about my looks and weight, dissatisfaction with anything I believe is mediocre, and a tendency toward workaholic behavior. Their influence is quiet but pervasive, reaching into all aspects of my life.

I'm sure you have a long list of such beliefs as well. When you look closely at them, you'll see that some of them contradict one another. Sometimes two contradictory beliefs are both true. Or both false. Or true and false at the same time. But we're operating according to these beliefs, whether they're true or not. They're alive inside us, influencing our every action, every conversation, and even *other* beliefs. It's no wonder we have trouble figuring out what we want or what we need to do!

Clearly, how and what we think can either expand our choices and opportunities or reduce them. We have so many beliefs, so deeply rooted, that it may be near impossible to tease out and define all of them. The best we can do is to know that those beliefs are there, know that some of them are false, and work on getting to the truth as best and as efficiently as we can.

Let's explore some of the things you were told, things you told yourself, and things you've come to believe—and examine whether or not these internal statements are getting in your way right now.

Exercise: Uncovering Blind Beliefs

- Make a list of sayings you've come to believe, including old sayings, advice, proverbs, spiritual teachings and bits of mother wit that you've heard throughout your life—the good, not so good, and neutral. Write down as many of these statements as you can remember.

- Next, think about the things you tell yourself. Write them down. These could be a thousand things. For example: I love to eat. I should exercise. I couldn't possibly go back to school. My head is too small to look good in that hairstyle. I am too big to... They would never let me.... I can't stop eating meat. I need a man who can take care of me. I need a woman to take care of me. I have to have my .... I can't just drink water.... I don't have time to exercise every day. You get the idea.

- Keep a journal and add to these two lists over the next few days. When the list feels complete, find a quiet moment to read through them, paying attention to your thoughts and feelings as you do so.

- Note which of these statements are obviously untrue, yet you continue to believe them as if they are true? Mark them with an F for false.

- Note which statements hold truth for you, even if it is something you have been in conflict or denial about? Mark with a T for true.

- Look over your list and re-read the statements that are true and those that are false. Think about how these statements are supporting or blocking the manifestation of your vision, consciously or subconsciously.

Uncovering and Questioning our Beliefs

The beliefs, statements, and fears that have gotten ingrained into our consciousness make themselves so comfortable that we're not even aware that they're there—much less that they're influencing our behavior so strongly. In my experience, most of us are holding on to beliefs that have nothing to do with our reality. It starts from the day we were born when our parents whisper loving advice in our ears. We continue to get them from our families, neighbors, and friends. Some of those beliefs also come from our religious texts, from our leaders, from society or from our life experience. They are things that someone told us we 'should' believe. And we did. We just accept them as truth because that is how we interpreted our experience. But while some of them are true and wise and have kept us safe, others only serve to get in our way. Much of what gets in our way is hidden in our subconscious. What you think—even if it's an unconscious thought—will manifest in how you act and experience life.

A boy let's call him Jeff, who is having trouble moving from learning to read to reading to learn, is told by the adults in his school that he needs extra help because he's behind. And, because he's been taught he should listen to grownups, he believes what they tell him. So he tries less because he believes, on a deep level, that they must be right: he can't get it. Instead of trying on his own, he waits for extra help. After a while, the help is not helpful and the helper begins to believe that the boy will never be able to read on grade level. The boy is labeled learning disabled. He interprets that to mean that he's stupid and it makes him feel ashamed, so he's motivated to do less and less over time. No one understands why he's getting more and more behind, because no one knows what is happening in his mind. They only know that he can't perform at the level that someone decided children are 'supposed' to perform.

Thankfully, Jeff's mother kept telling him a different story. Without her insistence that he *could* read, that he *could* learn, that there was nothing "behind" or "disabled" about him, he might have been totally lost. The stories she told him helped neutralize the story he was being told at school.

It's an all too common scenario—one that is familiar to many of us. I am sure there is something in your life that you were interested in but gave up on because someone said or did something that gave you a clear signal that you were not 'supposed to' want that thing, or be able to do that thing.

You may have noticed that the words 'supposed to' and 'should' are highlighted by quotation marks in these pages.

I want them to stand out for you whenever you read them or hear them because these words are clear signals that you are bumping into a block. Anytime you hear yourself or someone else say something is 'supposed to' be a certain way, let it be a sign for you to stop and listen very carefully to what is being said. You may want to ponder where that "should" statement came from and examine whether it is really true. Some 'supposed to's' or 'should's' are real and helpful. I found that 'being evenly yoked' in relationships is critical both in business and my personal life. My most successful relationships have been those where I and the other person were evenly matched in critical areas i.e. values, skills, philosophy, etc. Now, I pay real attention to this "should" and, as a result, I have more mutually beneficial relationships across all aspects of my life. You should not just reject a "should" out of hand, but really pay attention to the wisdom in the beliefs you hold. Examine those beliefs to see if they are serving you or creating blocks in your life.

Exercise: "Tell me about yourself"

Getting to the Current Truth

This exercise will help you practice checking out your assumptions, challenging your own beliefs and identifying your blocks. You'll explore some things you were told—and what you told yourself—to examine whether or not those statements are getting in your way right now. This is an activity designed to help you get in touch with your perceptions about yourself and your life by offering you a different physical experience to help you discover something new. Over the course of two days, you will be able to access parts of your brain that you don't normally use, as well as sort through your stories—both public and private—by writing with your normal (dominant) hand and then with your opposite (non-dominant) hand.

Day 1

Gather something to write with and some paper or your journal. Sit in a quiet place where you can relax and be free from the distractions of phone, media, people, disturbing noise or any stressful input. Take several deep breaths, inhaling and exhaling from deep in your body. Focus on your breath with the intention of freeing your mind of everything that is not related to this exercise. Now, write the story you always tell people when they ask you to "tell me about yourself." You may have several versions of this story, depending on the situation you're in. You may say one thing in a business setting about yourself and another when you meet someone you would like to get to know better socially. Any version will do for this exercise; simply pick one. Don't over-analyze what you 'should' write, just start with whatever comes to mind and stop when you feel it is complete.

Now, read the story twice. Take in as much of what you have written on as many levels as possible so you can understand what you have written. Let your story impact you intellectually, emotionally, physically, spiritually, etc. Then, make a list of what is true, and what is no longer true for you now or anything that feels like an incorrect perception in that story.

This exercise is intuitive. You just need to let whatever comes to mind come out without censoring. There is no right answer; the answers you're looking for don't lie in the story you actually write. You will simply learn about where you are in a different way than the public story you have been reciting. Take your time and pay attention to all of your feelings and thoughts beyond what you put on the paper. Take note of whether you're leaving things out, embellishing, or skipping over embarrassing tidbits. Sometimes we are in the habit of saying things because we have always said them. And we do it even when we have changed, and those things are no longer true for us and who we are. When you see a statement that does not resonate as a true representation of who you are, make a note of it. Pay attention to your story. Are you being overly modest? Are you gilding the lily?

Note: *Sleep with a pencil and paper next to your bed on the days you are doing this; you may have very vivid dreams that you'll want to make note of.*

Day 2

Again, sit in a quiet place where you can relax without distractions; free your mind of everything that is not related to your own progress. Now, with your non-dominant hand (i.e. if you are right-handed use your left hand and vice versa), write the story of your life again—this time write the story that feels really true for you now, not the thing you always say when people ask you about yourself. Remember to pay attention to any feelings or thoughts you have during the process. Now, read this new version of your story and think about the questions below. You may want to record your answers in your journal.

- How is your second story different from the first one?
- Why do you think the two are different?
- What has been useful or helpful about the first story?
- What does your new story reveal about how the first one gets in your way?

So now you have your own story and you may be thinking that you still don't understand how to analyze and make meaning of what you have written. As we grow, evolve and have different experiences—and we do that every day—we change. Our story has to change as well. And we can't just adopt new stories about ourselves without consciously letting go of the old story. If we aren't telling positive, powerful stories about ourselves, we may be inadvertently creating blocks.

Looking for Guarantees

There are many examples of how our thinking creates blocks that keep us from getting what we want.

Our society teaches us to rely on guarantees. And if you perceive your resources as limited, guarantees seem even more important and necessary. You don't want to blow what little you have betting on something that seems uncertain. We all want to know that, when we invest our time, energy or other resources in something, it's going to bear sweet, abundant fruit. However, I have learned how limiting that kind of energy and thinking can be. One of my mentors always says, "By the time the guarantee comes, it's done."

Stockbrokers will tell you the same thing. The time to get in on a lucrative investment opportunity is to invest when the company is new and untested; by the time the company proves itself and demonstrates success, the stock has already peaked. In order to take advantage of good opportunities—in any arena--you have to trust your instincts. So do your homework and learn about the opportunity or person. Then listen and trust yourself. Listen to the faintest whisper that says, "no this is not for you" or that says "yes, invest" (invest time, money, energy) in this opportunity or relationship. And do it without looking for a guarantee. These investments are faith moves, plain and simple.

One of the greatest obstacles is the need for guarantees. This is a big one for me. I hold back from making a move until I know I'm betting on a sure thing—though I know that there's no such thing. Every time that I think I have gotten over this self-limitation, I find a new way that I have held myself back while looking for a guarantee.

I have been taught, as most of us have, that we need some guarantee so that we don't get hurt or taken advantage of and so that we know our efforts will result in a favorable outcome. So, we ask lots of questions, we check references; we talk to others to see if they got what they expected and had a positive experience.

Take the story of a woman, I'll call Carol, an attractive woman in her early 50's who told me she was looking for a 'real' relationship. When I pointed out that she had someone in her life who loved her dearly, she rejected the idea that this could be her life partner. She said she wanted a man who could take care of her and make it possible for her to do all the things she dreamed of—travel, party, really enjoy life. The gentleman in her life, loving as he might be, couldn't provide that lifestyle for her because his current financial situation wouldn't allow it. She attempted to date him, but he wasn't reliable, she said. He often canceled plans with her because of work or family obligations. He didn't seem willing to put her first.

I asked Carol a question: "Why would he drop everything for you when you have made it clear—to him and the Universe—that he is not good enough? You are not willing to make a commitment to him without a guarantee." She was taken aback. It hadn't dawned on her that he might be hesitant to make a commitment to her because she had not made one to him. And as long as she was framing their relationship in terms of his inability to "provide" for her, their relationship couldn't progress. And she stayed stuck looking for the guarantee. If Carol could open her heart and make an investment of energy in the loving person in her life, she might find that she'd found a "real" relationship that was fulfilling—with or without the lifestyle she was hoping that a well-to-do man would provide her. Or she might find that with her commitment, he would be able to create the kind of wealth that they both wanted thus being able to provide her with her ideal lifestyle. And yet another choice for Carol might be to love herself so much her energy becomes a magnet for what she wants.

I was contacted by a young woman who was inquiring about a program in which I teach at the Gestalt Center for Organizational Systems Development. After I'd explained the program, she kept trying to get me to define what she would gain from it. I told her, "You will be better able to make a difference in the groups, organizations, and systems you find yourself in." That didn't satisfy her; she persisted. I told her that I didn't know her well enough to say *how* she would grow or what impact the program would have on her, but I could say that she would get what she put into the program and then some. She sighed in frustration. She wanted a guarantee. But she would have to sign up for the program and participate fully before she could ever know what she would get from it.

I've seen this happen with groups as well. The Catholic Church is going through a downsizing of sorts because of the lack of available priests and shrinking parish size. The churches in my region are in this process of "clustering"—combining parishes. When I attend these planning meetings and listen to parishioners' concerns, it is clear that people are afraid of losing the beloved communities they know and love. They seem very resistant to the change because they are questioning what the result will be, how they will get there and how they will fare in the end. But the process they are in is one of transformational change—no one knows how they will get there or what it will look like in the end.

I have been working to get ahead of my need for a guarantee for most of my adult life. I am just beginning to trust myself, my intuition, strategic thinking, and logic to the point that I am going after opportunities that feel right for me, but don't offer a guarantee. It feels really exciting and good.

It takes diligent self-awareness and self-reflection in every moment to retrain your thinking and move away from looking for a guarantee. Everything in our society supports, almost demands, that we look for guarantees, which makes this movement to inner knowing and trusting oneself, very counter-culture. Once you start to see yourself looking for a guarantee, then you need to examine your fear and reframe your inner dialogue. The difficulty is that there are dishonest people in the world. Discerning between doing due diligence and looking for a guarantee is tricky. So far, what I pay attention to is that fear feeling. If it is not present, then I am almost sure that I am doing the appropriate checking to discern if the opportunity is real. If that fear is there, I may still be doing the appropriate due diligence, but is it still likely that I am looking for a guarantee.

Playing the Skeptic

At a summit for minority- and women-owned suppliers, I heard a presentation by a company seeking non-majority suppliers. The company went to great lengths to share information about their upcoming initiatives and to be honest about what opportunities were still open and available for suppliers and what doors had already closed. Although it was a very positive event, some suppliers left the meeting feeling doubtful. They'd been to this kind of presentation before; they had heard this kind of rhetoric, only to find that the doors that they'd heard were open seemed only to be open to the same old suppliers that had gotten business year after year. Their experience seemed to indicate that no matter how many opportunities were promised; very few actually came to fruition.

Perhaps their skepticism was well-founded. Perhaps the company was not being as above board as it seemed. But, ultimately, what did that mean for the suppliers. Should they stop bidding for contracts? Should they submit perfunctory bids, just to test the waters? Should they try—again—to submit a competitive bid for a contract? If these suppliers were unwilling to abandon the skepticism and be open to the possibility that perhaps opportunities really were open this time, it's unlikely that they would make the effort to really go after one of these contracts. And that would guarantee that the door would never be open to them. Relying on old experiences could potentially block them from taking advantage of a new opportunity.

It's important to know how to allow your experience to inform how you listen and discern in a given situation, without allowing it to block the possibilities available. In each situation we encounter, we have choices. The choice for those suppliers was A) to wait to see if things had changed by holding back to see if some other company got the bid or B) to assume that the corporation was telling the truth about their efforts to make more opportunities available for new suppliers, and submit a competitive bid. Their success rested in the choices they would make.

Our choices, of course, have consequences that will impact our lives and the next set of choices available to us. Your work is to discern the choices in every moment and make the best choices you can to move you toward your vision and then have faith that the Universe will line up the next thing you need for your learning and the manifestation of your vision.

Minimizing Your Strengths

My public story for many years was that I was married to a wonderful man and that we were working together to make our dreams of having comfortable, successful lives come true. This was my vision—and my illusion. Although my husband was a good person at heart, we were not working on making our dreams come true as I dreamed and hoped we would. That was the reality—and it had nothing to do with the story I told myself.

And get this: Even when I made any significant step toward that successful, comfortable life I dreamed of, I played it down, especially to my husband. I did it to maintain harmony in our relationship, I told myself. Perhaps I subconsciously wanted to keep from damaging that all-important image of us as "equals" when it came to finances and power. I wanted to make my story true.

But I was blocking my success not only by my attachment to my "story" but by minimizing my potential and, in turn, the very energy that I needed to generate in order to manifest my vision. This was creating a push-pull kind of energy with the Universe that was neutralizing my efforts because I was saying in one breath, *Yes, I want it all,* and then in the next breath, *No, I can't be too successful, I will make do.* Pulling between those two opposing views was keeping me stuck in one place.

Eventually, I began to change my story. I stopped saying "I just want to make the rent" and started saying "I am powerful and successful and deserve to have all my dreams come true." The more I said this at every opportunity, silently and aloud to myself and others, the more my world began to change – for the better.

The Illusion of Doing It Alone

American culture has promoted the idea of the rugged individual who does everything by himself and for himself. Yet, when you listen to successful people talk about how they achieved their success, they always seem to be thanking the people who helped them get where they are. But I have heard countless stories of people who set out to pursue their dreams without consulting anyone with experience, and without tapping their network of people who might serve as positive resources, and without asking for help when things got difficult. These people struggled and failed because they felt that successful people were 'supposed to' do it on their own.

It finally occurred to me that this notion of "you've got to go it alone" or "if you want something done, you have to do it yourself" was a cultural myth or another American lie. No one ever does anything without help.

Asking and accepting help is very important for your success and for the success of the person offering help. It helps them. Asking for help is not a sign of weakness. It takes strength and courage to know when you need something and to know whom to ask and when to ask for it.

Acknowledging Fear

When I find myself putting up blocks, creating reasons why something will not work, questioning whether I am doing the right thing, I now know that something is scaring me. I am afraid. In fact, I believe the main reason that we don't get beyond the limitations of our thinking is that we are scared. Fear is the number one block.

In my work, I am often called on to raise money or help my clients raise money for their nonprofit organizations. People are terrified to ask people for money. They find all kinds of ways to avoid doing it for several reasons. Fear of rejection is primary. The truth is that three out of four times you will get no for an answer. It says almost nothing about the person doing the asking. This is just the way the process works. If you move beyond the fear that paralyzes you and keeps you from asking, then you see the pattern and know that you need to ask four times as many people to meet your goal.

In coaching situations, I have seen people sabotage themselves because of the fear of succeeding. They know what to do, they are very competent, and they get their thinking twisted and their knickers tied in a knot, only to find themselves experiencing exactly the thing they were afraid of.

The law of attraction is at work. You attract exactly what you think most. The Universe doesn't understand 'not'.

Our fears, while they seem very real to us, are often irrational. You are afraid to ask for a raise because the boss might say no. Well, what's the worst that can happen? The boss will either say yes or no. Nobody will die or get sick if you ask for a raise. The sky won't fall. The sun will come out tomorrow. You may even find out what to do to get the raise if you stay in the conversation and don't run away too fast.

A behavior I have developed when I am facing fear is to take a quiet moment and listen and talk to myself. I say, "Yes, I am afraid. What do I need to pay attention to in this situation? What do I have to do to move through this fear and make a move that propels me positively toward my vision?" This has been very helpful. Sometimes admitting that you are afraid, allowing yourself to feel it and learn what the fear is trying to tell you can be the most powerful thing you can do. Fear can be a gift of insight if you don't let it stop you from moving forward. It is like a traffic light that blinks a yellow caution signal telling you to be careful. Don't let fear become a stoplight that keeps you from moving forward on your journey. Do what you'd do when a traffic light is broken and stuck on red. Slow down, look both ways and move right through it.

Another way of making fear-less fearful is to think about how it can be your friend. For example, people used to always tell me how strong and courageous I was, especially after I started my own business. What they didn't know was that I started my business out of fear. I was more afraid of getting stuck in some dead-end job than I was of making it on my own. I was more afraid of what I would do with my regrets than I was of failing. This aspect of fear was actually helpful in making me reach for my goal.

Making it work

Over time, as I have accepted my own reality, and freed myself from the beliefs that didn't work or hold truth in my life, I realized that I could discover or create a reality that was unique and true to me, so that I could be true to my calling and to the people in my life. More importantly, I stopped holding myself back and limiting my potential by trying to fit into a mold that was not designed for me.

How did this happen? I kept talking to myself. Every time I ran into one of these 'supposed to' thoughts or when someone else tried to limit me with a 'should,' I'd start talking to myself about what I wanted. I told myself that I was not going to limit my efforts to accomplish my vision because someone said it was 'supposed to' be a certain way. I'd remind myself of the many ways I could accomplish my goal. And I would talk to other people who were positive and had worked through the things that limited them. They shared their wisdom with me freely, and many directed me to ask myself the important question: *What are you afraid of?*

In answering that one question, I would learn the next block that I needed to work through so I could get what I wanted.

There is one more thing that I do and that I ask others to do: *Be thankful.* Every morning as I open my eyes and every night as I close them, I list all the things that I am thankful for in my life. I call each person by name. Each act or action, each lesson, I list individually in detail. I remind myself of all the people who love me and whom I love. It often lulls me to sleep, as if I were counting sheep. And it keeps me moving positively forward.

> Try This:
>
> If being thankful is something you find difficult, try starting a gratitude journal. Each day, add to the list of things you are grateful and thankful for. Don't forget the little things: Every act of kindness you did or that someone did for you. Every courtesy. The value of the conflicts you encountered and how they got resolved or what you learned from them. Try to spend 5-10 minutes each day adding more things to this list based on your experiences that day. Read your list each day. Do this for 30 days and see what you notice about yourself and your daily interactions.

You Can Do Anything

Let's return to one of my personal beliefs that I listed in the Introduction: *You can have anything you want as long as you are willing to do what it takes <u>for you</u> to get it.*

Notice the emphasis on "for you?" Each person is different and unique. Each of us has gifts and challenges. If you want to accomplish something, it may cost you more effort than the next person. Each person has a different life experience that has affected their thinking and beliefs. What works for one person, won't necessarily work for someone else.

We want so many things. But moving from desiring something to acting on that desire is no easy task. It's risky because it requires that we take a chance and that we work through (or work with) the fears that are blocking us. When given the opportunity to act on those desires, we see where our commitment is. Many things can happen. Often times, we: 1) find that we are not willing to do what it takes; or 2) we bump into a block, shut down and don't know what to do next, or 3) we become clearer about what we really want and redouble our efforts to get it. Getting through the blocks that we or others create to our vision is part of the journey. Are you willing to do what it takes to get what you want? That is the question.

Exercise: Identifying Blocks

You have created your vision and your current reality. Make a list of what is standing in your way, what is blocking you from having your vision, your ideal lifestyle right now.

Now, read over your list. This is where you start to make changes in your thinking, your behavior and your world.

CHAPTER 5: DIRECTIONS – CREATING THE ROADMAP

A goal without a plan is just a wish.

For any dream to become a reality, you need a plan—one that will effectively support you in moving from where you are to where you want to be. At this stage of the game, the focus is on setting direction. This is where the rubber meets the road and things get mapped out in a realistic way.

Setting the direction for any road trip is an important part of getting to your destination. Determining the direction or strategy for your Life Map is the next step in mapping your future. Strategy is what gets things moving forward. I define strategy as *key actions that take your blocks and current reality into consideration and move you towards your vision or ideal lifestyle.* Ideally, strategies are catalytic and help you move ten giant steps forward, instead of one baby step at a time.

Strategic questions

In order to develop a strategy, it helps if you can discern your "strategic question." A strategic question comes out of sitting with all the information you have generated so far: your vision, current reality, SWOT, blocks. The strategic question helps you discern how to leverage all of this information. It is the question that unlocks the door to your movement and makes everything fall into place.

Discovering or developing your strategic question is key to developing a direction that leads not only to the career, financial or personal goals that you desire but that creates the opportunity for you to live your ideal lifestyle.

For example, I once coached a University professor who also had a consulting business. Delores wanted to do her consulting work full-time. She wanted to have the option to teach without the responsibilities of University life—serving on committees, politics, etc. She wanted to be able to keep the financial security of having a full-time job, i.e., a steady paycheck so she didn't have to change her lifestyle. Her strategic question: "What is needed to stay connected to the University and move to consulting full time?" Ironically, her answer became the very thing she didn't want to do - retire. By buying a few additional years into the retirement plan at the University, she would be eligible to retire early, collect a regular paycheck and spend her energy full time on her consulting business.

A couple that I coached discovered that, on a certain level, their current circumstances actually were supporting their living their ideal lifestyle. Jan and Juan were graduate students, lived at a private school in exchange for some light maintenance, had three children and both picked up periodic organizational development work and teaching opportunities. They wanted to live in simple yet beautiful surroundings, be able to put their family and children first, and surround themselves with wonderful people. They had all this even though they did not own their home. And, they wanted to do work that was fulfilling. Their teaching and organizational development work was very fulfilling. Yet, they wanted more financial security for themselves and their family. This was the missing element.

The traditional idea of getting jobs as they finished their degrees (Juan was working on his Ph.D. and Jan on her master's degree) was not going to support their lifestyle and their desire to have time, energy and attention for their children. Their strategic question became "how to find meaningful work and a path to financial security while maintaining their ideal lifestyle?" This became the focus of our work together.

Notice that we are calling this the *strategic* question. This isn't about just asking a bunch of questions that are going to have you turning in circles, unable to determine which way to go. You will need to frame one question in such a way that it will lead you to a clear answer. This is where care must be taken.

A guy is driving along a long country road in the middle of nowhere and has a flat tire. When he gets out to change the flat tire and he realizes he has no jack, so he goes off in search of a jack. He framed his problem as "I need a jack to change the tire and I have no jack. Where can I find a jack?"

Another car, coming down the same, lonely road has a flat tire. The driver of that car discovers he has no jack either. But he frames the problem as, "I need to change the tire, I have no jack." The strategic question is: *"What can I use to lift the car so I can change the tire?"* He looks around and sees a log and a large rock, which he uses to lift up the car and change the tire. He continues on his way, passing the first guy still walking down the road--still in search of a jack.

By framing the strategic question as "how do I lift the car?" instead of "where can I find a jack?" the second man opened himself up to many more choices about how he might solve the problem. This is true with strategic questions in Life Mapping. They are best framed in ways that offer you options, choices, and opportunities. Often, we have preconceived notions about what the answers to our questions will be, so we may build the answer into the question or subtly anticipate the answer before we even ask the question. We're not really asking a question at all. We certainly aren't asking in a way that enables our minds to be open to the multitude of possibilities that might frame the answer. That's what happened to the first driver. He thought he knew the answer to his problem: *I need a jack.* A more open-minded approach to the problem might have led him to a different outcome.

Usually, strategic questions are framed to address a few key issues that don't go together. In the first example, the professor/consultant had three things she was paying attention to:

1. Financial security
2. Quitting her full-time job and still being able to teach

3. Wanting to consult full time

Delores opened herself up to exploring how these three ideas can come together through clear action to move her closer to her vision. From the answer to your strategic question, you can move to action.

- ***Moving to action***

For me, strategies are key actions and they have some simple criteria. Strategies are action-oriented, forward-moving, and they make effective use of your resources.

- ***Action-Oriented*** strategies include things you can actually do. They are things that you have control over. For example, paying into the retirement plan so you can retire early, or looking for a job, or consulting opportunities that give you time to spend with your children. The idea of putting your entire future into winning the lottery doesn't seem like a great strategy unless you can count on working the science of numbers and really calculating what numbers, in what frequency, you would have to play in order to actually give you the best odds of winning.

- ***Forward Moving*** strategies are actions that get you closer to your vision in very tangible ways. Strategies should allow you to do something every day that advances you toward your goal. Each day you can decide what are you going to do that moves you closer to your vision now.

Note: *In the beginning, it may be easier to take small steps in line with your strategy, especially if you are venturing into something that is new for you. For example, I've known for some years that I wanted to publish a book. I knew I was a fairly good writer, but I felt I hadn't done enough writing for public consumption. First, I recommitted to writing regularly in my journal, just to get used to writing again. Then I began to look for some small, safe opportunities to publish. I started writing small feature articles for my neighborhood paper; then I moved up a notch and wrote an essay that was published in a professional journal. I realized that I was writing all the time for my clients and began to value that writing and publishing of reports to clients as valid writing. I wrote a more formal paper with a colleague who had a track record of being published and we presented it at a conference.*

I joined a group dedicated to culturally-based work with communities of color, and together we developed a writing project that will soon become a published book. Before long, I had a better sense of my writing abilities and could better envision myself writing a book. And along the way, I began writing this book in earnest—one idea and one chapter at a time. The small-steps approach requires patience and dedication, but it's a good way to keep yourself from being overwhelmed by your own vision.

- ***Resource Leveraging*** strategies use what you have at your disposal in a way that maximizes the power of that resource. How do you leverage your resources? It's not always as simple as "when you have lemons, make lemonade," but that is the basic concept. Leveraging your resources is mostly about remembering what you know, what you have and who you know. So often we forget what we have as we pursue the next thing we want. So looking at your current reality can be helpful in discerning what is available to you right now that will move you toward your vision. How many times have I bought a white shirt to wear with a suit only to clean out my drawers the next month and find three other white shirts similar in style? Often, we know people who do the very thing we need to have done, either a business service, home repair, or something that we begin looking to have done when the Universe has already introduced us to that person in preparation for this moment. Networking is a great example of using what you have. We all have people in our lives who have hidden or not-so-hidden talents that could help us in our own goals. People are often quite willing to share their expertise, skills, talents, and experience to help others.

Networking Tips

- Talk to people you don't know
- Find out what they are interested in, what they do and what they need help with.
- Tell them what you are looking to do, what you are good at and what you need help with.
- Think about and suggest who you know that is interested in or able to help them
- Always follow up, say thank you and keep your word.

Use networking to find the information and expertise that you need.

Thinking about strategy

There are other things that you want to consider as you begin to plot your direction and develop strategies about how to get moving.

1) ***What are the requirements for achieving different parts of your vision?***

There is an entire process and criteria for becoming a doctor, which includes an undergraduate degree, medical school, internship, residency, getting a medical license, and finding a place to practice. Other professions have their own set of requirements. You need to know what they are and what the process is for meeting them before you decide to hang out your shingle. And if you want to be a family doctor in a small community, the requirements are different than if you want to be a renowned cardiothoracic surgeon at a major research hospital.

If your goal is not a career goal, there are still requirements. If you want to retire at 50, you need a means by which to support yourself for the rest of your life. If you want to live in another country, you have to find out what the immigration policies are, figure out how to find housing and work, learn how to speak the language and so on.

The main question here is "what must I do?" What do you have to do to make your vision real? If you don't know the answer—say, you're not sure what kind of license you need to start your bed-and-breakfast—then finding out becomes your first task. Thanks to the internet a great deal of information is at your fingertips. Government websites, industry associations, other resources can help you understand the industry, hobby or causes in which you are passionate. The internet is also a good place to find out who else is doing or involved in your passion.

Then there are your personal requirements. You may say to yourself, "I want to own my own business and I want to maintain the lifestyle that I have achieved for my family while I was working my regular job." Your strategy will address this dilemma of how to have both sides of this requirement.

2) What will it take for you to meet the requirements?

The emphasis here is on what *you* are willing to do. There may be general requirements for meeting a goal that someone else could easily meet, but that you might find quite difficult or be unwilling to do. Every person is different. Some people are good at math; others are good at baking.

Everyone has a different skillset and a different set of circumstances that will affect his or her ability to do any given thing. Creating an effective strategy requires that you honestly assess your strengths and weaknesses to determine what it will take for you to make your vision real. You also have to look at what you're actually *willing* to do. Then you can commit to what is required and create a strategy to match what you are willing to do to get what you want.

Your commitment is important. You cannot imagine how many unhappy people I have met who are upset that they haven't attained their dream, yet they have not been willing to do what it takes to get there.

If your vision is to be the head of your own company, but you also want balance and to be able to spend time with your children, you have to understand what it takes to lead a company, see how that might affect having time for your family, then create a strategy that is likely to allow both. Some women have brought their children to work while they were infants. Other women I have read about telecommute or job share. Finding out what others have done or what your options are for managing your dilemma is the beginning of creating a powerful strategy.

This was my dilemma. I wanted to run a company, but I also wanted to be near my kids. My strategy was to start my own company and work at home. When my children were small, I kept a home office and I stopped working from 3:30 to 9:30 in the evening in order to be a mommy and do the after-school shift. After the kids went to bed, I went back to work until about midnight. There were plenty of pros and cons. I was able to be my own boss. Having a home office also kept my overhead low, gave me a tax break and was an efficient way for me to work. The downside was that my company could only grow so much with me working a split shift so to speak.

The exercise below will support you in creating your first set of strategies.

Exercise: Strategic Actions

This is a strategy development exercise designed to support you in uncovering what you need to do next to bring your vision closer to reality. You will build on your discoveries in the SWOT exercise and the other work you've done up to this point.

Materials:
20-25 index cards

Instructions:

1) Think about your vision and your current reality.

2) Taking your current reality into account, brainstorm 15-20 actions you can take to move towards your vision. Each idea should be an action you have the ability to implement. Don't worry about if it's a good idea or not, just brainstorm freely.

Note: *You may not be used to brainstorming. Brainstorming is generating as many ideas as you can without judging them as practical, doable, good or bad.*

3) Write one idea on each index card. Be clear and concise. Eliminate extra words and be sure you will understand what this card means six months from now.

4) Group the cards based on the actions that are similar. This could mean actions that can be done simultaneously or all the ideas that require a certain type of action. For example, you may have three cards related to getting training or increasing your education. They would be grouped together.

5) When you are satisfied with the groupings, give each group a name that will capture the essence of all of the actions in that group. This name should be an action phrase and contain an action verb that is the summary or big action for that group of small actions listed on the cards. Something that you can keep in your head, work on every day and that will guide your decision-making. A summary or a big action for the three cards might be "increasing my skills through education". The naming is important because these will be your strategies. You need to understand what you mean and be able to see how to move into action with these summary actions on the cards. So, "increasing my education". I might be clear that this means taking workshops on becoming an entrepreneur, or computer software like QuickBooks. The names of these columns will frame how you approach moving toward your dreams – they are your strategies. Make them positive and action-oriented, forward-moving and/or resource leveraging statements.

6) Use the chart at the end of this chapter to capture your ideas and strategies from this exercise. Put the names of the groupings on the top row of the chart and the other ideas in that group in the column underneath.

7) Ask yourself the following questions:
    - What words or phrases stand out about the actions and strategies you just created?

- What comes to mind immediately about how you can begin moving forward?

Make some notes to capture your first thoughts as you look at the work from this exercise, so you don't lose any good ideas. Pay special attention to where your thinking goes and what your uncensored reactions are. Keep those observations for later as often this becomes valuable information when you begin to run into blocks to your vision.

After you have completed the sorting process in the previous exercise, look at your strategies and see if there are any column names that are repetitive or can be succinctly combined without losing their impact. Ideally, you will have between 1 and 6 strategies—a manageable number of big actions that you can remember. This will force you to decide how you really need to focus your actions and energy. And they will fit nicely on a card or in your PDA or cell phone so you can keep them with you and refer to them often.

Now brainstorm some small steps under each strategy. These will be the first steps to implementing your strategies. Some of the original cards may become part of this list; some of your notes from other exercises may become part of this list. New ideas will come to you. You will begin to see new opportunities as you get more into the process of working with your strategies. Don't hold on to your first ideas in a rigid way. Stay open to what is available and how you, your environment and others are changing. Use the chart below to capture your strategies and action steps.

Strategic Actions

Strategy:	Strategy

Strategy	Strategy

Why Strategy – Another reason

Strategies are a tool to help you stay focused. The value of having a Life Map strategy is that it helps you to stay on your path and see opportunities when they present themselves. It is a simple way to stay focused on what needs to be done.

It also helps you know when to say 'no' and pass on opportunities that don't support your progress. For example, as an entrepreneur, I meet a lot of other people who own or want to own their own business. Many of them have chosen businesses that are based on a tiered marketing model like Mary Kay, Warm Spirit or VM Direct. They are very excited about their opportunities and they want me to partner with them because they see me as having an expansive network that would support their businesses. In their eyes, it would be a win-win situation because it would make money for me as well.

Because my strategies are clear, I can say no to their lovely offers because I know they would create a detour on the road to taking my company where I want it to go. I also know how much energy it takes to market and manage my own business. To veer away from that to work on something that's unrelated to my work is not something that I need to do. Being clear that these opportunities don't serve me, enables me to graciously say no, but it doesn't preclude me from offering them support in ways that make sense for me.

There is so much going on in the world, so much information and misinformation that it is easy to get off track. My hope is that armed with your strategies, you will have a tool to make every day count towards the journey to making your vision real.

So, now you have your vision, your current reality, and your strategies. Sit with this accomplishment a moment before moving on to the next chapter.

CHAPTER 6:

ON THE ROAD – IMPLEMENTING YOUR STRATEGY

No matter how small and unimportant what we are doing may seem, if we do it well, it may soon become the step that will lead us to better things.

Usually, when my family goes on a road trip, I'm up half the night before getting ready—packing, cleaning, cooking food for the trip, checking the weather and reviewing directions. I want to make sure we have a wonderful trip and that we are able to get in the car in the morning and get to our destination the way we envision. I spend the time and energy because I want to be clear about the route I'm taking, the time it may take, what I'll need along the way, and what I can expect to encounter. I don't want to get on the road and realize that I've forgotten something critical, so I envision the trip and plan and prepare. But you can't prepare forever. Once I've done all I can to get us ready, there's nothing else to do but get on the road and see what happens.

You have been getting ready for the most exciting road trip of your life. You've clarified your vision, worked through blocks, explored your current reality and analyzed your own thinking to see how your mindset is supporting and blocking your progress. You've come up with some strategies that will chart the direction to your vision. You have a direction. Your life map has been charted. Now it's time to put your foot on the gas and get moving. The next step in Life Mapping is implementation.

The next step in Life Mapping involves setting priorities about: What you want to do first?, How fast you want to go?, How you are going to attend to the journey and the destination? The exercises in this chapter will support you in creating a 90-day action plan. You'll also have a checklist that, like signs on the highway, can help you to know how far you have gone and how many miles to your destination, where the rest stops are and what sights you might choose to stop and see on the way. Creating a vision helps you determine the destination, but we're about to begin the journey—and the journey is the fun part.

Do What You Can Do

How do you know where to start? Which thing should you do first and how do you decide? The best choices are based on your understanding of how to get from point A to point Z. I know a real estate agent who had a lucrative hobby of buying and renovating houses. Bobbie was successful at it because she had the process down to a science. She could close on a house and remodel it in about four to six weeks—before the first mortgage payment was due. The key to being able to move this efficiently is in knowing the best way to sequence the process. If you have the right plan and execute it in the right order, you can avoid delays or "redo's" later. In this case, for example, she knew to schedule the floor tile guy at a certain time, so he was not in the electrician's way. But she didn't know this the first time she rehabbed a house. It took some trial and error, some investigation and consultation with experts. All of these are action steps that eventually brought her to peak efficiency and effectiveness.

Other processes are not nearly so linear. For instance, in writing this book, I created my vision for the book first. I started out by just writing down my ideas. I put things in order later. I knew that if I worried about the order, I would get stuck. My priority was to get moving so that I wouldn't get in my own way by getting mentally trapped. The lesson: Sometimes you just need to take the first step; put things in proper order later.

When I did my Ideal Day exercise, I saw myself doing tai chi and yoga out on the balcony outside my bedroom. Well, at the time, I didn't know Tai Chi nor did I have a balcony. I could have decided to wait for the balcony, but my first step was to buy a tai chi video and start practicing in my living room once a week. That was my way of putting my foot on the gas—getting on the road headed in the direction of my vision. A few years later, I bought a house. One day during the purchase process, I looked up and my eyes filled with tears as I realized that my bedroom had a balcony. My dream was being fulfilled.

Start with what you can do now. Pick what makes sense to focus on now. The rest will come when it is time. **One note:** Pay attention to procrastination.

Sometimes it's more important to leave the kitchen dirty and work on that resume or business plan or give the children the extra attention they need than it is to get everything on the list done. If you find yourself doing everything else but your priority task, stop, sit with your feelings and see what you are afraid of that is keeping you from doing what is really needed. I often fall into the "I have to wash the dishes first before I can start writing my book" syndrome. Sometimes it is procrastination because of fear, sometimes it is that thoughts and ideas are marinating and need a little more time to gel. Now, I can stop for a moment, check-in with myself and see what is going on – then make a conscious decision about what I am going to do.

Turning Baby Steps into Giant Steps

We have talked about how strategy allows us to take ten giant steps forward through a single action. That's important, and we shouldn't minimize the smaller steps. There is value in baby steps. The old adage, "Don't bite off more than you can chew" is applicable here. Taking on too much at once can cause you to be overwhelmed—and that's a block in the making. At the same time, you don't want to be too timid. You want to move with an appropriate amount of speed and a certain amount of flow. If something feels too big, you can start with a small step and work forward in a way that keeps you moving as you wait for other things to fall into place. Moving is moving, so whether you're taking large steps or small ones, you are ahead of where you were—and much closer to your goal.

Unless you are super motivated, capable and all the

stars are aligned just right for you (which is entirely possible), often it is helpful to break giant steps into smaller strategic steps. Your giant step might be to become a movie screenwriter. One of your baby steps might be to write a screenplay and get some movie credits. Your actions might go like this: 1) get more information about the movie industry, 2) take a class on screenwriting, 3) attend a film festival, 4) ask the writers you meet how they got started; 5) volunteer on a film project. Do what you can today and you will begin to see and to figure out what you need to do tomorrow, next week and next month.

Do something every day toward your vision. Those baby steps will add up over time and begin to look like giant steps.

Right now, let's look at each of your strategies and think through the giant steps and the baby steps or action steps that will get you moving toward implementing those strategies and manifesting your dreams and goals.

Exercise: Thinking Through the Giant Steps

Instructions: In this exercise, you want to think about the key actions that will get you moving on each of your strategies. What are the big actions or giant steps that will move your strategy forward?

Fill in the chart below, writing your strategies from Chapter 5, page 89 in the first column. Then in the boxes next to that strategy, write one to three giant steps that will get you moving.

Strategies	Giant Steps—Taking Action		
Example: Become a screenwriter	Example: Take screenwriting course to learn the craft and meet others in the business	Example: Build relationships with others in the film industry via a local film festival	Example: Get film credits by volunteering on a film project (don't forget to negotiate credit upfront)
One			
Two			
Three			

Now, look at your Giant Steps. What are the baby steps within each of these big actions? Let's break that chunk down into a few bite-sized pieces that you can begin to act on each day.

Say your giant step is to run a half-marathon. When you begin to train, you won't want to start the first day by running ten miles. You have to run short distances and build up your strength and stamina. You want to start with small actions so that you can work up to the big actions in a sustainable way.

The pacing is important. You want to make small changes consistently. My friend, Liz, now in her mid-fifties, trains for triathlons. During the winter, she tries to swim once a week and do yoga. When the weather is good, she walks. After about two weeks, she starts running, increasing her distance each week until she is running five miles two or three times a week. As it gets warmer, she starts riding her bike, going a little further each time until she gets to her goal. Then about three months before the race, she starts putting those activities into the same day's workout—running, biking and swimming so that she continues to build up her stamina without burning herself out.

Looking at the exercise above, think about the steps you have chosen to make. Are they manageable steps? Do you need to break them down further? What is a good pace at which you can accomplish these tasks? How will you keep yourself motivated? How will you keep yourself consistent?

Tips for Staying Motivated and Accountable

1. Create a chart for your progress
2. Reward yourself at key milestones in your progress with celebrations or treats
3. Post motivational saying and affirmations in key places to encourage you to keep going, i.e., bathroom mirror, bed stand, desk, refrigerator
4. Post your goals for the next 90 days where you can see them

Make That Change

My triathlon friend, Liz, is a positive model for changing or adopting any new life habit. Remember, changing your behavior is not easy. It took you years to develop your current habits, and years to develop the thinking that keeps you doing what you are doing. To make substantial and lasting changes, you have to change your thinking as well as your actions. The steps you take—small, consistent modifications—will eventually become the fabric of your new life.

Sometimes you will have to leave your old habits and activities behind gradually, making room for the new habits and practices. My advice to budding entrepreneurs has been to keep your day job until your business creates enough income and takes so much of your time that you don't have *time* to go to your day job. This may not take very long if you're able to get your idea or company up and running quickly. Or it may take several years and require extraordinary patience to create a situation that would allow you to leave your job and still take care of your personal and family responsibilities.

Only you know your situation and your level of risk tolerance, so your strategy for moving into your ideal lifestyle will be different from anyone else's.

Street Maps – Following those baby steps

One of the main reasons people get stuck is because they don't put enough detail into the goal or action they set out to achieve. The exercise that follows will help you create the "street map," a more detailed action plan so you will know just what you need to do when you get off the main highway. It will give you a way to integrate baby steps (small actions) into your daily life so that you are always moving toward your vision. It creates a way to assess whether what you are doing is working overtime. This detailed, structured action plan can provide you with daily action steps so that you don't have to think about the "what's" and "when's"; it's laid out for you. All you need to do is follow directions.

Exercise: Creating a90-day Implementation Plan

Instructions: Fill in column one with the giant steps from the chart in the previous exercise. Then think through and write two actions for each strategy that you will commit to doing each month in the next 90 days. It might be a daily, weekly or one-time action that will move your life map forward.

For example, you may write down that you'll make an appointment to meet with a specific person who can help you reach your goal or provide some information. Or you may say that for 90 days you will get up 30 minutes earlier and exercise. There have been times when I simply committed to reading or researching something on the Internet, or making three calls per week to potential clients. Keep it realistic and doable in the context of your life and responsibilities at home and at work.

If you want to make dramatic life changes, explore the implications of your desires by taking into account the very real issues of money, family and business relationships, as well as your personal assets and challenges.

To work through the transition, you may want to talk with an objective person who is both positive and successful. One of my clients, I'll call her Mary, wanted to earn more money as a consultant, but she found that she was not able to get herself to do all the things she thought she should do to move towards that goal. In reality, there were things she didn't take into consideration—namely, her obligations to her daughters and her granddaughter took a considerable amount of her time. She realized that she could renegotiate her obligations with her daughters so that she could free up more of her time to concentrate on her business.

Mary also had a major internal block—fear of rejection or not being loved. The two issues were connected. As we explored the time management issues, the fear of rejection came up over and over again. It came up in the many ways she said 'that won't work' which pointed to her fear that her daughters' anger was a threat of rejection. We talked about the fact that a deep-seated belief like that would take time to work through. It was scary for her to set boundaries with her daughters and in business with this fear of being rejected lurking in the shadows. Together, we designed a few small actions that would push against that block a little bit each day. We worked to undo the belief that she would not be loved or that she didn't love her daughters if they were mad at her.

She created an affirmation and said it daily for 90 days. She found small ways in which she could set boundaries with her daughters. She made a baby step goal to network with one person each week that could be a potential client without the intention of asking them for business but simply for them to get to know each other. Each of these small steps was designed to enhance her growth as a consultant and create small actions that would move through a major block to her vision.

A word of caution: Don't make this too complicated. You know yourself. If you only commit to one action that you will do for the next 30 to 90 days, write it down and just do that. If your vision and timeframe require that you make lots of changes now and you are committed to doing that, the chart in this chapter may be filled. I would suggest that you not create too many action steps simply because you want to pace yourself to manage the changes that are happening in your life. You want to create a track record of success by not over-committing, especially in the beginning. You will want to allow yourself some flexibility to deal with the unexpected. What is possible and reasonable will be different for each person. In addition, you will need to identify the activities you are doing now that do not support your vision for your future and make some clear decisions. You are in control of your dream and how you move forward.

The worksheet you end up with will be a guide for your 90-day implementation plan. Put it on the bulletin board in your office, on the mirror, on the fridge; save it into your cell phone or PDA or in your calendar. The idea is to look at it each day and incorporate the action steps into your daily routine.

STRATEGIC ACTION	1ST MONTH		2ND MONTH		3RD MONTH	
3 strategic actions from the previous exercise you plan to work on for the next 90 days.	ACTION 1	ACTION 2	ACTION 3	ACTION 4	ACTION 5	ACTION 6
DATE ACCOMPLISHED: WHAT I DID TO CELEBRATE:						

STRATEGIC ACTION	1ST MONTH		2ND MONTH		3RD MONTH	
3 strategic actions from the previous exercise you plan to work on for the next 90 days.	ACTION 1	ACTION 2	ACTION 3	ACTION 4	ACTION 5	ACTION 6
Strategy 1: Increase revenue for growth Giant Steps 1. Build new partnerships 2. Increases marketing 3. Life Mapping	Contract with one new partner Schedule meeting with potential clients	Redesign website	Edit Life Mapping Manuscript	Redo company profile Meet with potential clients	Edit Life Mapping manuscript	Host new TV talk show on public access for professional organization start taping
Build infrastructure for administrative efficiency Giant Steps: 1. Hire staff 2. Solidify & document process 3. Expand skill base of staff	Develop job description	Revise client and subcontracting agreements	Get referrals for administrative assistant position	Document processes	Interview potential administrative assistants	Document processes
Strategy 3: Manage household and children so family needs are met Giant Steps 1. Hire afterschool and overnight childcare 2. Get tutoring for kids 3. Exercise 30 minutes/day	Keep cleaning service once a month 30 min day on treadmill – keep log so you don't lie to yourself	Organize kids to do chores other 3 weeks	Post tutor/child care position at local college	Until childcare is available schedule 2 hours a day with kids to do homework like it is a business meeting	Hire child care/tutor	Monitor chores for effectiveness
DATE ACCOMPLISHED: WHAT I DID TO CELEBRATE:	Reward: eat out on Fridays					

To receive a copy of these Strategic Action Plan worksheets, go to https://mossgransberry/90dayactionplanfreedownload-handout/

Using the Universe

All of the work you have been doing in creating a vision for your ideal lifestyle and then a strategy and plan of action is key to propelling yourself toward your ultimate vision. And then stuff happens. Sometimes it gets in your way and has to be worked around. Sometimes its good stuff—an unexpected opportunity comes up, for example, someone drops out and your name is next on the list for the promotion. These unexpected gifts and challenges from the Universe are what make it important that your plan is flexible and alive. If you become rigid or too myopic in your thinking, you may miss the synchronicity being created around you and thus the opportunity for the Universe to support you and your goals. So work toward your vision by creating a map that you can follow—and stay open to the unexpected gifts, coincidences, and opportunities that are unexpected and that will put you in the express lane towards your destination.

Get Ready, Set, Go

Now you have developed an action plan for the next 90 days that will help you become more focused in your actions so that you can see how you are moving forward. It will help keep you accountable and keep you from forgetting about what you want because you're too focused on the everyday obligations of your life. I get so excited for you when I remember what it was like at the beginning of my own journey.

CHAPTER 7: TURNING SNAGS INTO STAIRS – STRATEGIES FOR OVERCOMING OBSTACLES

Timing is everything.

There are times when things just don't go the way we plan. Something unexpected happens and causes us to have to detour from the path we'd mapped out. Our timing is off and a door to an opportunity closes. We experience delays caused by other people, circumstances or by our own blocks and procrastination. Or we make every possible effort to achieve our goals and... it just doesn't happen. When things don't happen the way we plan, we often get angry about the situation and blame ourselves for "failing."

We question our commitment and our abilities. Sometimes we even question our purpose. But delays and detours are inevitable on any journey. We are moving in this Universe along with millions of other souls—all of us at different places on different paths. It stands to reason that there would be traffic jams and flight delays; that we would be slowed because of someone's construction project; that we would be grounded because of foul weather.

In this chapter, we'll discuss some strategies to help you continue to move forward when things don't go as planned. The first thing to learn is that snags aren't stop signs. (Yield signs, perhaps, but not stop signs.) And there is always more than one way to get what you want. In this chapter, we will explore ways to practice asset thinking, find alternate routes, recognize different kinds of spiritual "traffic" signs and know when stop really does mean *stop.* We're going to practice the kind of affirmative, analytic and out-of-the-box thinking that is needed in order to overcome the obstacles that stand in the way.

Embracing delays

In writing this book, as eager as I was to complete it, there were times when I needed to put it down to attend to other business obligations. There were times when I was delayed by the people and circumstances around me. I had to remind myself that this was okay and that I might even learn something important for the book by taking a break. There were other times, though, when I told myself, "*You need to make time for this book even if it means putting other things on the back burner.*" I continued to change the printing date with each delay.

Sometimes delays are the Universe's way of telling us that we need to slow down and look around a bit before we move headlong toward our goal. You may have experienced a situation in which an annoying delay turned out to be in your best interest. (I think of the people who worked in the World Trade Center who were late for work on September 11, 2001.) When you find yourself held up despite your best efforts to move forward, it is time to stop, sit still, take a breath, and look around to gain some perspective. If you've done everything you can, there's nothing else to do but watch the situation unfold and be ready to move as soon as the way is clear.

Sometimes snags result from our own inaction or procrastination—and that is often rooted in fear or some other kind of block. Discerning between external delays and internal blocks—and figuring out how to work through them, either way—is the work of Life Mapping. You can identify external delays because in order to get things moving you must get another person to do something. Internal delays require you to shift or change something in yourself.

The important thing is to look for an opening that will allow you to move forward even if it is only one step. Sometimes one step will get the energy un-blocked.

There is always a lesson to be learned from a delay or obstacle regardless of the source. One way to move forward in a good way is to ask the question: "What is the Universe teaching me at this moment? What is the lesson I need to learn in this situation?" This question will allow you to detach, get the lesson and free your mind to see a way around, over or under the obstacle.

Getting Up Instead of Giving Up

I coached a fellow entrepreneur and writer who had a grand vision of a grand book tour for her recently self-published book. She was eager to experience the lights and glamour of her vision. She was not ready to do what it would take to implement that vision. First, the need for sponsorships, the cost of hotels, and the timelines for decision-making became clear realities to her. Her advisors questioned what she thought she could accomplish with no capital and only a few months planning. In unison, they all advised her that this would not work.

And she and I talked through the choices and possibilities of accomplishing her intention in a more realistic manner. I encouraged her to check her hidden assumptions about the people she hoped to partner with and what they would bring to the table in terms of sweat equity and support. Ultimately, she took the advice she was given and developed a realistic picture of what was possible for her. She scaled down her vision to something she could herself manage with her current connections and resources. This was more palatable to her than delaying her tour for six months to a year while raising money for her grand vision.

The point is this, in the face of all the feedback she was getting; she could have abandoned her ideals. That's what a lot of people do—just give up when they hit a snag. It's easy to go right into a negative thought mode: *Oh, this is not for me. I can't be successful at this. These things never work out for me.* It's certainly easier to stop and turn around than it is to climb the mountain that has appeared in front of you.

Sometimes our plans don't go as well as *planned,* at least not the first time, but that doesn't mean that you're on the wrong path, or even that you have to go back to the starting point. You just have to know how to look at your situation and discern how to keep moving forward as positively as you can. This was what my star-struck writer figured out. Instead of giving up, she used her strengths; she scheduled a series of visits to cities where her friends were very involved with their churches. She held talks and small workshops with back of the room book sales in those cities without incurring hotel or audio/visual charges or having to feed people. She simply had to get there. That was in her budget.

Creating a Life Map keeps you so focused on the goal and makes your vision so clear that you really want to keep going, even when things don't go the way you imagined. Your vision, your ideal day, your values, your strategies, your 90-day action plan, your affirmations are the tools that help you stay on the road to your ideal lifestyle. It is when you hit a snag that it is most important to pull out those tools and use them as a lifeline to pull yourself back up and get back on the road.

Through obstacles, you have the opportunity to learn valuable lessons—if you pay attention to what you're learning from the experience. You also have to move away from judging yourself as bad or good because of these experiences. And you will learn a lot about yourself, too, as you make powerful choices to overcome the setbacks, to keep moving and not get stuck. Your Life Map will support you in getting the insights you need to make choices that will move through the obstacles on your journey and to keep you motivated to move forward.

Saying "no" to "no"

Experienced salespeople—whether they're selling cars, magazine subscriptions, Avon or Amway—eventually learn that "No" has many meanings:

- I don't understand the value of what you're selling.
- I don't have the authority to make the decision.
- I don't have time to think about it.
- You've approached me the wrong way.
- I'm embarrassed to admit I need this.
- I'm afraid to say yes.
- It costs too much.
- Maybe—in six months.
- Yes—if you jump through some hoops.

A good salesperson will tell you that if you address the underlying issues behind the "no," you can often turn "no" into "yes". Sometimes "no" means you need to change your approach or your presentation, to get a "yes." You may need to objectively evaluate how you are coming across to people to determine if there are changes you can make that would make your presentation more appealing. Always ask for feedback—and listen to it carefully. People will often be very frank and honest with you. It is in these moments that your self-esteem, your determination, and your commitment will be tested because you will have to move your ego out of the way in order to hear and respond to honest feedback.

Sometimes it's your hair color, your skin color, your stature or your accent that is getting in the way. In that case, you may decide that the 'yes' is not worth it. Most of the time, however, when you experience rejection, it has nothing to do with a judgment about you; it has everything to do with the person saying 'no'.

Sometimes a 'no' is the way that the Universe saves you from an unnecessary negative experience. It may be making way for you to have a more positive experience with the person who understands your vision and approach. Yet, there are times when 'no' just means 'no'.

My grandmother used to say, "When one door shuts, another opens." And for some of us, we have to find the open window, mail slot or vent in order to get in. I took her wisdom to heart. When I didn't get cast in shows in college, I produced my own. When I wanted to write this book, publishers and literary agents didn't understand my vision, I started my own publishing company. I was determined not to let anything or anyone get in my way—including me.

I had many a stern talk with myself about my procrastination, my fears, my priorities, and my expectations. In the self-help world, they call it positive self-talk. Whatever you call it, it works. Eventually, I found myself editing the last chapters, reviewing beautiful cover art, and laying out pages. I could happily say, "Soon!" when people asked me when the book would be out.

Asset Thinking

When you hit a snag, it's helpful to do some asset thinking. Asset thinking is the practice of looking at all the things that are available to you that can help move your vision forward. These may be resources such as money, information, people, ideas, location, opportunities. Your assets may lie in a previous experience, your sunny personality, your unique skills, even your looks.

I remember a dancer I met when I was a summer apprentice with a small dance company in Washington, DC. Johnny gave me my first lesson in asset thinking. He was not a great dancer—imperfect feet, poor technique, poor extension. But he had a presence—and he knew it. He'd always say, "If you give upper body, no one will look at your feet." And he was right. If you observe almost anyone you would consider successful, you will find that they have used some attributes that others might consider a weakness. They have either turned it around to their advantage or put the spotlight so squarely on their assets to the point that their weakness barely gets noticed.

By focusing on what you have to work with instead of focusing so much on what's missing or lacking, you can begin to see more possibilities and be inspired to keep moving. Your assets can propel you forward even when the odds are against you. Asset thinking is a very valuable practice for strategy building and problem-solving.

<u>Exercise: Practicing Asset Thinking</u>

The purpose of this exercise is for you to practice 'asset thinking' in a very simple way.

Brainstorm a list of positive attributes you possess right now, even if you cannot see how they may be related to your vision. Pick one item in your vision to focus on for this exercise. Now, look at the list of assets you have generated. Circle the assets that would be an obvious help to you on this aspect of your vision. Place a star next to the three assets least likely to help you move forward. Now, write a fictional story about how you make this aspect of your vision come true in the next three days using the most obvious assets and the most unlikely assets. Be as creative and outrageous as you can.

Reflection: Read and reflect on this fictional account of your success. What did you do with your obvious and unlikely assets? What did you discover about those assets? How can you apply this to your real-life situation?

Alternate Routes

Kathryn's desire was to help people. She worked hard to become a scientist in the hopes of making an important discovery. She spent long hours in the laboratory, writing up her findings and publishing articles on her research. She taught at a university. After many years, she found herself unfulfilled. She had grown tired of being alone in the lab. She wanted to do something new and different. At about that same time, her husband got a job opportunity in another state. She left her university position and followed her husband. In their new city, she began looking for a job. She made the decision to shift careers. She searched her heart and realized that she wanted to work with people, have flexible hours, and find a way to help others realize their dreams. She became an insurance saleswoman specializing in annuities and life insurance.

Kathryn was able to get clear about her intention or life's purpose—to teach and to help others. She was able to find a new mission, a new way to accomplish her life's purpose that was more in line with her ideal lifestyle and vision.

I hope that you are learning how to see new choices that can help you reach your destination. Being able to see an abundance of choices is important. That way when you wind up at a dead-end, you will be able to see the footpath that leads through the woods to the next road. When you run into a major construction site, you can retrace your steps and find a new choice that keeps you moving forward. When you have an accident or even get knocked down, you will have a way to get back up and keep moving towards your destination.

Personal Review

When you run into snags in your life plan, it may signal that it is time to do a personal performance review. We're used to having performance reviews at work. (Nobody likes them, but we're used to them.) And when they're done well, they can be very helpful in enabling an employee to assess his progress, his strengths, areas that need improvement, and future prospects. The best performance reviews also set goals and expectations for the coming year. A personal review gives you the same kind of information, but it can encompass all kinds of personal and professional assessments.

In fact, it's useful to periodically do personal assessments whether we run into snags or not. It will help you determine whether you've created the Life Map you need or a map based on some lie you've told yourself or some truth you haven't been willing to face. If you base your future on a false ideal or an incorrect self-image, your map won't have the kind of impact it could have. Being honest with yourself is vital.

Being honest with yourself is also difficult. You probably don't experience yourself as others experience you. We all have blind spots. Discerning who we are and how to be our best self is difficult. Our egos are invested in having us see ourselves in a certain way. The good news is that most of our flaws and faults are simply human—forgivable and reversible.

Ask other people to give you honest feedback about some aspect of yourself that you have questions about. If you listen carefully to what others say about your impact on them—and listen without judgment of them or yourself—you can discover blind spots or areas that you may want to change. It's a challenging process, but it's all in the name of getting what you want out of life.

One of my clients, Karen, was about to get fired because of what boiled down to a power struggle with her boss. She'd started to believe that her manager had it in for her, that he wanted to control her, and that he wanted her to act like his previous assistant. Her resistance to his suggestions came out of her need to establish herself as her own person and her perfectionist nature. She recognized that her predecessor, although very accommodating, was not following procedures. Now, she was cleaning up their mistakes.

When I first met with Karen, I listened to her story. She talked about her stress and anxiety about work. She talked about her boss, how much he was monitoring her every move always wanting to know where she was, and how critical he was of her relationships with other staff members labeling them as being 'too' social. I asked her if she wanted to keep her job. "Yes," she said, "At least until I can get a transfer."

"What do *you* need to do differently to change the interaction with your boss so you can keep your job?" I asked. Together we did some brainstorming. We discovered that keeping her job and feeling at ease there required her to make sure her boss felt appropriately taken care of. It had never occurred to her that he wanted to be able to protect her from other naysayers in the department who were approaching him. She had not put herself in his world where he needed to prove that he was running a tight and efficient department. We discussed those behavioral tendencies and their impact on her relationships on the job. Karen tended to be focused on accommodating others and helping them with procedural issues that they didn't understand.

Then we assessed which of those traits, skills, and assets she thought she could use to support her boss. She came up with three things that were simple enough for her to do, that didn't make her feel like she was changing who she was just to please him, and that would enable her boss to feel informed and comfortable that projects and tasks were being accomplished.

When she was able to see things from a different perspective, it helped her to reevaluate how she approached the situation. I encouraged her to view the situation from her boss' perspective, consider how to maintain her position, and to look at alternatives that she had overlooked during the emotional struggle with her boss. Her emotions had clouded her thinking. She was not being completely honest with herself nor was she able to hear the feedback her boss was giving her. She needed help to effectively evaluate her own behavior and open her mind to make room for other points of view, not just the story she'd told herself.

<u>Exercise: A Quick Self-Evaluation of your Life Map</u>

Instructions:

1. Review the strengths and weaknesses that you outlined earlier in the SWOT exercise.
2. Are they accurate? Are there other things that need to be considered?
3. Review your vision—can it be more clearly articulated?
4. Have you really been honest with yourself?
5. Use the chart below to evaluate your Life Mapping process and how it is serving you.

How am I doing with my Life Map?	What is working	What needs improving	What needs to be different
Vision			
Current Reality			
Strengths			
Weaknesses			
Strategy			
90-day Action Plan			

Creating and Co-Creating

There is a Universal Law that says we are all actually working *with* the Universe as a co-creator of our experiences. A power that is greater than us, that we can't see, can't prove and somehow are comforted to know exists—is present in every moment of our journey. And with each thought, word, and deed, our energy is joined by this Universal energy in the co-creation of the world in which we live. It's comforting to know, that you are never left to your own devices, isn't it? Even when no one seems to be there for you, the Universe is organizing itself to give you what you have asked for.

In order to experience the miraculous loving energy that supports our very existence and answers all of our longings and desires, we only have to pay attention to it. And we have to pay attention to what we "feed" it.

We have to be careful how we think and move, and be mindful of what we ask for and pray for because the Universe will begin to organize itself to give us that very thing. Because the Universe reflects our energy back to us, it helps us manifest whatever we put forward—positive or negative. The good news is that, if you've asked for something that isn't working for you, you can ask for something that will work. You and The Universe can change your world to suit you.

This is important when you are dealing with snags. As you move with your Life Map, the world and 'road conditions' will change. You will get new information about the world, the direction you were going or about yourself. This new information may require that you change your vision or direction in some way that will offer you a better way to achieve your ideal lifestyle. By asking the Universe for what is needed now, you can shift the energy and begin to attract the new thing that is needed.

When the Signs Say Stop

Yes, you should strive to overcome obstacles. Yes, you should look for the doors of opportunity. Yes, you should tell yourself you can do what you want to do—and you should believe it. Go for what you want. Go hard.

But know that there are times when you must heed the stop signs. If, after careful thought, analysis and contemplation, you feel you have misread or mislabeled your vision—or if you change your mind and want to head in another direction—stop and regroup. If something just feels wrong in your heart and soul... stop. If something hurts physically or emotionally or is damaging in any way to your spirit or the spirit of others, by all means, stop.

Something to Think About -
Be aware of triggers to past traumas or hurts.

Sometimes after you have been hurt or abused, you need time to heal. During the healing process, you may be suspicious or easily triggered emotionally or extra sensitive to the way you are treated. This is normal. Be aware of your feelings and triggers so you can discern whether you are at risk of a repeat hurt or if you are simply fearful. Watch your actions, reactions and other people's actions, to discern what is real and what is an illusion.

You may be moved to change direction because you've made some sort of inner leap. As we grow, our vision of what we want in life changes and shifts. As we begin to achieve some of the things we have envisioned, sometimes our vision changes. What we thought we wanted isn't as satisfying as we believed it would be. Perhaps that nursing assistant who dreamed of shopping all day long would find herself bored with retail therapy and longing for the excitement of working in the hospital again.

Sometimes life makes you stop. This is what happened to my dear friend, Alice, who was stopped when she broke both her ankles and was restricted to her home for six months. During her convalescence, she had to stop taking care of everyone else and let others take care of her for a change. And she finally made time for her art and her jewelry making with renewed energy. What may have seemed like an unfortunate delay turned into a great lesson and opportunity for her.

The beautiful thing about being human is that you can change your mind and you can change direction. You can stop anytime. And the other amazing thing is that you never really stop. You may slow down, you may become completely still—but the world is still turning and as long as you're sitting on the planet, you are moving forward. Stopping one thing in one way may really be moving you swiftly toward something else. Every ending is the beginning of something new.

Exercise: Asset Thinking

The exercise will help you to reframe perceived threats and obstacles into a positive statement of your assets. To begin, draw a line down the middle of a piece of paper to make two columns. In column one, make a list of any obstacle or deficiency or situation that appears to keep you from moving toward your dream. Make the list as long as you like. In column two, write the opposite of what is listed in column one. At first, just write a short, objectively opposite statement. Then spend some time thinking about how this "opposite" might actually be true. Take your time. Changing a negative belief into a positive statement of your assets is a paradigm shift that is not always an easy one to make. This is practice, the more you do it the easier it will become.

Example:

Not enough money	I have money. Right now, I have $8,456 in my bank account, which is enough to pay my bills for three months.
Not enough time to do everything in the day	I have 24 hours in a day. I can choose to spend that time on what is important to move me towards my vision
Not enough confidence to go out and really sell my services	I am confident that I can sell. I can increase my confidence by making one sales call a day
Too worried about guarantees	I can live without guarantees. I can surrender my success to the Universe so that I won't create the need for a guarantee
Lack of resources	I have resources—books, contacts, information, my mind, my heart, my computer, the internet, my friends and colleagues, etc.
Don't have to access to the right people	I have strong relationships with smart people. My existing relationships can lead me to other people who can help me achieve my goals.

The most powerful way to change our world is to change our minds. The value of snags is that they challenge us and offer us the opportunity to change the way we think. When we change the way we think, we change our world. It is our choice to make our corner of the world a better place.

Chapter 8: Living and Loving Your Life

Use your strategic positioning and the resources you have now to build solid relationships, help others, and create mutually beneficial opportunities for yourself and your network.

Mapmakers constantly update maps—removing towns that have withered away, renaming streets, expanding borders, drawing new highways. A map isn't a static thing—it's not carved in stone like Moses' tablets with the Ten Commandments. The map you make for your life is a flexible one. It will change as you change and grow. Now that you have created this life map to guide you and keep you on the path that you have chosen, it is important to remember to regularly take a look at how the journey is going.

Even if you have already begun to see some of the benefits of Life Mapping, it's important to remember that this is not a quick fix or a temporary assignment. This is a life-long process. You will want to ask yourself some questions—and seriously consider the answers—as you come to different junctures in your life. Are you enjoying it? Are you headed in the right direction? Are you attracting the people and resources into your life to make the journey meaningful and enjoyable? How is the world changing and what do you need to do differently so that those changes don't have a negative impact on your life? What are you setting in motion that will support you and your family for the next seven generations? Depending on your answers, you may need to change your plans—revisit the exercises, revise the responses to the questions, rethink your approach.

Once in a while, the signs are big and loud like a billboard or neon sign saying, "Get out". Twice in my life, I have had that experience. Most profoundly, I was living in Atlanta and after the 1996 Olympics, I had this overwhelming feeling that we needed to get out of Atlanta. I couldn't explain it to anyone's satisfaction. I just knew I had to leave and ultimately, I realized that I needed to move to Cleveland, Ohio. It made me sound a little crazy because I had never been there, my parents had moved there a few years before. It was one time that the message was so powerful that I didn't question it; I simply did a little research and started packing.

But most often, I find that the messages for change are whispers or passing thoughts that can easily be overlooked. Once I started to track those whispered messages, whether I followed the instruction or not, eventually I learn to listen and obey. Just like the guarantee, once I understood the message and what was behind it, it was over. Sometimes, it is as simple as, take your computer and later I find out what I needed the computer for. Sometimes it is to go the back road, or stop at the store, or go back home and get something or call someone. Timing is everything. You never know what the Universe is lining up for you.

While you are living and implementing your life map, it is so important to keep your map current, manage change, get out of your own way, shapeshift, and stay on course.

Keeping Your Map Current

The world is changing constantly—and those changes will have an impact on your life and may you too take alternate routes. When something major happens—you or a spouse is laid off or downsized; when an elder parent can no longer live independently on their own; when a child graduates from high school or college; when a loved one becomes incarcerated, struck with disease or disabled—the picture of your current reality changes and adjusted must be made. Life Mapping can be a tool to support you moving through these life's changes in ways that are optimistic, movement-oriented and uplifting.

You will also change and evolve, as well. Although your purpose and the essence of who you are, will remain the same, your goals and the way you view the world when you are 25 is vastly different from those at age 45. So, you may find that, as your interests and priorities change, you may want to change your goals, your strategy or your approach.

In any case, it won't serve you to stick to a plan that no longer works or to keep going in a direction that's clearly a dead end. And certainly, if new information, new technology, new resources become available that can help you move more efficiently and with more peace and grace, it would make no sense for you to stick stubbornly to your old plan. Incorporate this new-found assistance.

There are several ways to keep your map current:

1. Revisit your vision – periodically take time to read and re-visits your vision, making any adjustments that are needed.
2. Check yourself and your environment for new blocks and obstacles—continuously tracking and learning about yourself as you go along throughout your daily activities is a great way to identify blocks and obstacles and keep them from stopping your progress.
3. Develop new strategies - annually or bi-annually revise the strategies and approaches in your Life Map.
4. Create a new implementation plan annually—use the worksheets or some format that works for you and work your 90-day map.

For more than 30 years now, I have taken time each December and each summer to revisit my Life Map. I revise my current reality and review my vision to see if I need to add or delete anything. Change can happen so profoundly and so quickly that it can be difficult to recognize. You have to work at staying conscious of the changes so that you can keep up with them. At one Life Mapping workshop, a participant asked me to share my Ideal Day. I was about to launch into my traditional ideal day when I realized that my life had undergone several changes. My children were older and more self-sufficient. My husband and I had divorced, and a new man had entered my life. I began in that moment to revise my ideal day to incorporate my teenage children, my new man and the new vision I had for my company and my life.

Every year, I review my strategies, redoing the relevant exercises keeping my new vision and current reality in mind. Sometimes I find that my original strategies are still valid. At other times, I realize that the strategies need to be altered to accommodate changes in my environment and new opportunities. For example, not long ago when I looked at the vision I had for my business, I realized how changes in the economy and the marketplace were affecting my business. As the field of consulting is becoming more crowded, the competition for clients has increased and the need to distinguish my company from others has become increasingly important. This awareness motivated me to adjust my Life Map as it pertained to my work and create a new business plan even though my current business plan was only two years old.

Implementation and action plans must be reviewed as well—and probably more often than anything else. Your implementation plan is the most dynamic part of the Life Map. You will probably find that your action plans shift like the Hogwarts stairs in Harry Potter. Even if your priorities and strategies are not altered, your implementation process may change, depending on changes in your circumstances, resources, new knowledge or other factors.

The good news is that with change, comes new opportunities. With a retirement or downsizing, comes the opportunity to move into a new career that is closer or more fulfilling than the one before, and a chance to use old skills in new ways. A child moving away from home may mean more intimate time alone for their empty-nesting parents. An elderly parent moving in may present an opportunity for adult children to develop a new bond with their parent.

The most important part of any change is your attitude. The way that you view, think and talk about the changes will have an effect on your experience. Looking for the opportunity or silver lining in change, and finding ways to release attachments to what was, are key to moving through change in a good way and being able to keep moving forward towards your vision.

Getting Out of the Way

The biggest challenge many of us face is keeping a handle on how we might be getting in our own way. It's definitely a challenge for me. As soon as I think I have finally overcome some deep-seated block, it morphs and finds a new and more subtle way of seeping into my thinking and my actions. Many of our personal challenges are so deeply rooted and so much a part of our way of being in the world, they are difficult to see objectively. They sneak up on us and foil our plans before we know what happened.

Shape-Shifting

Information is power, but only when you use it or respond to it effectively. When you add new information into your plans and strategies, the ground shifts under you and you have the opportunity to become something new. A few years ago, when I was creating a new business plan, all the research I found seemed to indicate that the most logical strategy for expanding my company was to pursue government contracts. There seemed to be lots of opportunities on the federal, state, and local levels. So, for two years I laid the foundation for pursuing these contracts, getting certified and preparing to make bids. At the same time, I began to network and attend conferences related to minority business development; I got involved with my local Minority Business Council and got active in some other professional and became active in business organizations where I was already a member.

The next thing I knew, I was building a powerful corporate and entrepreneurship network. Business opportunities started coming my way—but not from the government. I realized that this was the Universe at work supporting my intention to expand my company, but in a way that was much more accessible and expedient than government contract opportunities and with a lot less paperwork and politics.

When I realized what was happening, I shifted my strategy to make government contracts secondary and corporations my primary market. I am still riding quite successfully on this strategic shift. I didn't abandon my efforts to obtain government contracts, instead, I accepted and responded to the new information that showed me that building my corporate practice first would serve me better in the long run and get me to my destination faster.

Staying Focused on Purpose

For me—and for many of us, I believe—it always comes back to purpose and mission. We want to understand our reason for being on the planet and we want to fulfill that purpose. By consciously focusing your energies on your vision, Life Mapping helps you stay on purpose.

My purpose at its core is to make the world a better place. I share this purpose with many other people, but my particular way of doing this is by helping others see the choices they have so they can free themselves. My personal purpose and mission permeate through everything that I do in life—my actions, my interactions with my loved ones, and my work with individuals, groups, and organizations. My life map has served me by helping me to find clarity about how to accomplish my purpose and live my ideal lifestyle. Every day I am living my purpose and making my vision real, decision by decision, choice by choice. Staying on purpose happens each moment of each day. Use your Life Map to guide your decision-making and to discern the choices that will help you accomplish your purpose and live your ideal lifestyle.

True to the Journey

Life Mapping is a transformational journey. We have a choice about how we travel on that journey. What we do with our circumstances, how we make meaning of life's events and whether we choose to enjoy the process all depends on us—our attitude and our approach.

There are a few things that you—that all of us—would do well to remember as we travel along our journey.

- Keep your mind open and be flexible. You don't want to lock yourself into (or out of) a situation.
- Listen to your instincts or intuition—the voice inside that says, "call her now," "drive by the house," "stop," "slow down," "something has changed," "wait."
- Stay awake. Be aware of all that is going on in your world and the greater world in which we live. Change is moving at a faster pace than ever before. We're bombarded with "information" from every direction—and much of it is unreliable. It means we must ask more questions and pay as much attention to what is *not* said as to what *is* said.
- Be ready to shift. As you see changes, make adjustments in ways that keep you moving positively forward.
- Exercise your prerogative to change your mind. If things are not going as you would like, if you start getting what you asked for and it's no longer what you want, stop, let go, take time to get clear about what you want now, change your direction, and start on a new path.

Life Mapping has transformed my life. I am truly happy, I am constantly becoming the person I want to be, I love myself, I am manifesting everything that I need and want, and I am seeing the miracles and experiencing the grace and blessings of the Universe both in my life and in everything around me.

I hope that you will begin to change your thinking, treat others with kindness and walk with the positive mindset that you need for your vision to become real.

I hope this book will help you to explore your inner self and find ways to be kind and gentle with yourself and others.

I hope that this process will help you to be clear about what is most important to you and help you create that for yourself.

I hope that you will find be flexible enough to grow and change as the world shifts, yet never give up your right to choose.

I hope that you will find ways both small and large, to enjoy the journey.

I wish you peace, blessings and safe travels as you find new ways to make your vision real.

The Next Step

It is my joy to share all the ways I have manifested my vision and ideal lifestyle. This is regardless of the weather, the economy, and despite what others have thought or said. By focusing on how I want to live and how I want to feel, it has become a way of being no matter the situation or environment I find myself in.

When Everett & I made the commitment to spend the rest of our lives together, we went through the life mapping process together. This gave us a joint vision of our lives together and created a structure for us to truly support each other. Then we created a 5-year plan that outlined what we needed to co-create with the Universe to manifest our vision.

Over these 5 years, we have had many adventures. We have also manifested everything we agreed upon. And new things have come into our lives that we never expected to bring us the lifestyle we have been dreaming of creating.

Our commitment to focusing on what we want to create and moving in every way we can towards that vision has kept us on track.

This year, Everett retired from his day job and has come into my business. Our working together and traveling together for business and pleasure is the joy of our lives. He loves the coaching work and is as gifted as I envisioned. We are committed to sharing Life Mapping with you and others. To that end, we have launched a learning community to support those who want to go deeper in this work. We are excited to invite you to join us.

You can find more information at
www.mossgransberry.com

About Monika

Monika Moss-Gransberry, Author, Self-Mastery Coach and Consultant

"On my life-long journey to wholeness, I have used many methods to get there none more important than Life Mapping. I have found my purpose and that is what led me to write the book, Life Mapping: A Journey of Self Discovery and Path Finding. Life Mapping is a life-enhancing process that leads you to live the life you always dreamed of but never thought possible. I am living my dream and I am happy and I am at peace. And every day, I get to help others do the same. As important as my 30+ years as a consultant and coach, is that I am a living example of what life mapping can do for you."

For 30 years, master mapper and business consultant, Monika K. Moss-Gransberry has dedicated her talents to helping organizations and individuals create powerful road maps to their vision. As founder and president of MKM Management Consulting, Monika is committed to partnering with others to make a difference by supporting the transformation of individuals and organizations.

Life Mapping has guided Monika in overcoming life's obstacles and creating a road to success, happiness, and joy. She has supported thousands of people to map their future and make their visions real one leader, one organization and one community at a time, transforming organizations and building the capacity of individuals who live in them.

Her certifications include Gestalt practitioner, certified facilitator by the Institute of Cultural Affairs and National Coalition Building Institute. Monika is a published author of

- Life Mapping: A Process of Self Discovery and Path Finding
- The Technology of Doing Creating & Being (www.mossgransberry.com) and,
- Contributing author for Embracing Cultural Competence (www.embracingculturalcompetency.org) for which she received the 2009 Alliance for Nonprofit Management Cultural Competence Award.

She has taught at Cleveland State University, Fordham University, and a graduate of Howard University, Columbia University, and Leadership Cleveland (2007).

She is currently on the faculty of

- the Gestalt Organizational and Systems Development Center (http://www.gestaltosd.org),
- The Goldman Sachs 10K Small Business Initiative (http://tric.edu/workforce/GoldmanSachs/Pages/default.aspx), and
- Move the Crowd Academy (http://www.movethecrowd.me).

www.ingramcontent.com/pod-product-compliance
Lightning Source LLC
Chambersburg PA
CBHW072348090426
42741CB00012B/2971
9780984952021